Lake Tahoe's Desolation Wilderness Fishing Guide

Jerome Yesavage

ABOUT THE AUTHOR

The author started trout fishing fifty years ago in the eastern United States. He spent many years engaged in technical rock climbing in Yosemite and the backcountry Sierra Nevada. Over the last thirty years he has explored the Desolation Wilderness, systematically fishing each of its over 100 lakes while maintaining a cabin in Tahoe City near the Truckee River. Proceeds from this work will be used to encourage membership in California Trout, where the author is currently Chairman of the Board of Governors, and champions continued efforts to maintain such fisheries as the Desolation in the future. Dr. Yesavage is also a professor at Stanford University.

He maintains a web site on fishing the Desolation http://www.stanford.edu/people/yesavage/Desolation.html and (usually) responds to e-mail questions and other comments about the fishing (yesavage@stanford.edu). Reports to this web site and by e-mail are essential to keeping up with the evolution of the ever-changing fishing in the Desolation. They will be even more important in the future as management adapts to the situation in the lakes and streams.

The author on summer vacation 1972.

ACKNOWLEDGEMENTS

Since the first edition of this book published in 1993 the author has maintained a web site to receive fishing information about the Desolation. This new edition includes the information gleaned since 1993 and will attempt, through continued electronic efforts, to keep up to date with the fishery as it evolves without fish planting.

Many of the people who contributed information and photos to this book we at CalTrout consider "streamkeepers" of the Desolation, i.e. those who have a personal commitment to preservation and enhancement of the piece of California fishing heritage they treasure. I cite some personally, while others would prefer to remain anonymous and others yet have changed their e-mail address and appear lost in the ether. Also thanks a lot to the overworked Department of Fish and Game (CDFG) biologists Mitch Lockhart and Stafford Lehr who provided much information for this work.

The scenery photos of Gilmore and Half Moon Lake are by Brianne O'Rourke and obviously the Lake Trout of Gilmore are by the Wakabayashis. Dr. James D'Andrea, took the glider shot of the Meeks Creek lakes. The Tyler grave photo was taken by Tom Hoffman who saved me a long walk. Mitch Lockhart provided the great CDFG frog photo. The remaining photos are by the author, taken with a Canon ES10, or 40D. The film shots of the brookies and browns, used Fuji Velvia film and were "push processed" two stops. This is the procedure championed by one of the greats of color outdoor photography, Galen Rowell, resulting in highly saturated colors perfect for fish.

Finally, I also acknowledge the many donors to California Trout from Tahoe and elsewhere who enabled us in 2008 to establish a field office in the Lake Tahoe area with professional staff. Peter Spain has allowed us to use his incredible Tahoe photograph in this effort (http://www.peterspain.com).

The cover: Entering the Desolation Wilderness from the Fallen Leaf Lake trailhead on the trail to Triangle Lake. Fallen Leaf Lake, Lake Tahoe and the city of South Lake Tahoe are seen in the background, by Danielle Yesavage.

TABLE OF CONTENTS

INTRODUCTION

ORGANIZATION OF THE GUIDE

In addition to the Introduction, this guide is organized into **seven chapters, each referring to a particular section** of the Desolation Wilderness. In general the sections follow main stream drainages with specific information about each fishable lake in that drainage. Since most trails follow these streams there will be little information about hiking other than to mention the names of the appropriate trails.

Several excellent topographic maps are available of the area. The map to have is the "Guide to the Desolation Wilderness" produced by the U.S. Forest Service. This 1990 creation is highly detailed with a 2" to the mile scale and 40' contours. It is hard to get lost with it. There are also excellent hiking guides available. Probably the best is Robert Wood's Desolation Wilderness but this book is long out of print. Its detailed treatment of cross-country routes is worth a library search. Less detailed but more up-to-date and available is Jeffrey Schaffer's Desolation Wilderness and the South Lake Tahoe Basin. The new book comes with a map.

HISTORY

It is important to note at the start that the Desolation Wilderness represents a large fishery, a complex fishery and one with a long history. The geology of the area is ideal for producing small glacial lakes in granitic basins. There are over 100 such lakes and numerous streams. In the earliest days there were rainbow trout in Rockbound Valley, descended from steelhead in the Rubicon River. There were also the Lahontan cutthroat trout of Lake Tahoe which worked their way up tributaries into Fallen Leaf, Cascade and Floating Island Lakes. Man, of course, encouraged movement of fish into barren areas of the Wilderness even in the last century, with the first recorded planting occurring in Gilmore Lake in 1887. A major effort was made by members of the Mount Ralston Fish Planting Club (MRFPC), formed in 1925, who over the following years planted over 100 locations in the Wilderness. This group also led the building of modest streamflow dams on 23 lakes to stabilize waterflow in creeks below lakes, so that fish might spawn in the streams and survive dry summers, especially when the lowest flows occur in the fall. In the 1950s the California State Department of Fish and Game (DFG) began planting by aircraft. The last major planting occurred in the 1990s, after which planting in the High Sierra was severely restricted to protect the Mountain Yellow-Legged Frog and limited to a very few selected

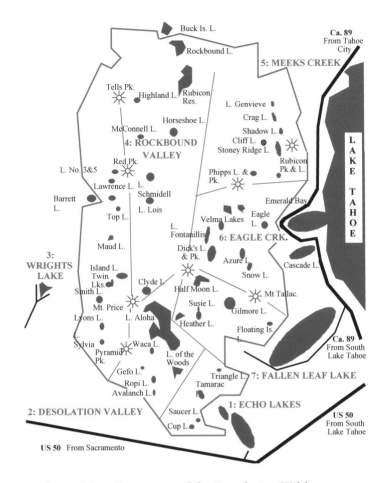

Seven Main Drainages of the Desolation Wilderness

lakes. Thus, to all intents and purposes the Desolation Wilderness is now a "Wild Trout" fishery.

In the last few years attention has focused on whether planting has been a good idea in the overall management of Wilderness. Issued raised have included whether or not planting contributes to overuse and whether or not trout have had an adverse effect on certain native amphibian populations in the Sierra such as the Mountain Yellow-Legged Frog (MYLF). Despite such concerns there has been little hard data gathered about the biology of these fisheries and man's impact. The proceeds from the first edition of this book were used to help fund some biological studies of the area by the California Department of Fish and Game and the United States Forest Service. These studies defined the residual populations of frogs in the Wilderness, mostly on the western side of the Wilderness. During this period of time there have been a series of legal challenges to planting in the Wilderness and it is currently severely curtailed.

4

THE SPECIES

Until the stocking efforts of DFG the Desolation was basically an eastern brook trout fishery. Although today the most common species remains the brook trout, there is now a wide variety of fish in the Wilderness. Useful references for those interested in more information about species from a genetic and biological perspective include Trout Biology by Bill Willers and Inland Fisheries of California by Peter Moyle.

Brook Trout (BK)

The handsome main actor in the Desolation, the "Eastern" brook trout

The most likely species of the trout you just caught is a brook trout or "brookie". This "trout" is not really a trout but a "char" and is native to the eastern United States and Canada. There are many wildly colored different char found in Arctic waters. The fish is dark green or blue-black on the back, fading to white on the belly. Male bellies may turn a brilliant red in spawning season. The most distinguishing feature of this trout is its upper body markings which are worm-like or mottled. Spots on the side may be yellow or pink with blue halos. These are "light spots" on a "dark background". The lower fins including the tail have distinctive white leading edges. The tail is squared-off, not forked.

The main feature of the brook trout which led to its wide introduction in the Desolation is its ability to spawn in lakes without tributaries, which most the rest of its relatives listed below cannot do. The particular strain of BK inhabiting the Sierra was developed by Seth Green in the 1800s and is noted for its early sexual maturity, which has led to overpopulation of some lakes. Overpopulated lakes produce "stunted" fish with small bodies and oversized heads. One does not "Catch and Release" in such lakes. It is rather hard to overfish a brookie lake. Happily, these are probably the best tasting of the Sierra trout.

The expert on fishing the brook trout in California is John Wakabayashi. John, a geologist, has been all over the Sierra and maintains a useful website: (http://geocities.com/johnwako@sbcglobal.net). On his site you will read tales of "monster brookies" and where you might find them.

Rainbows (RT)

The typical rainbow with damsel flies paying a visit. Adult damsels, but more likely the nymphs, are an essential component of any flybox loaded for the Desolation.

The rainbow trout is native to some areas of Rockbound Valley. It can be identified most readily by the pink streak on its side; however, this characteristic is variable and may fade in lake-bound fish, which become more silvery such as those seen in Lake Tahoe. The back of the rainbow is usually olive to greenish blue and the belly is white. Irregular spots are found on the back, sides, head, dorsal fin and tail. These are "dark spots" on a "light background".

Some lakes in the Desolation have been consistently planted with rainbows and they have done well. RT spawn in streams and hence may be found anywhere that a once-planted lake joins a stream system. For example, they can be found in the stream than runs past Glen Alpine Spring, along with a variety of other species. Steelhead are ocean-run rainbow trout and at one time probably existed at the head of the Rubicon River. The Eagle Lake variant of the rainbow has been planted in several lakes in the past and is known for its strength. For all the years these fish have been planted in the Desolation, when one catches a 'bow here it is likely to be a genetic smorgasbord.

Large fish have been found in Stony Ridge Lake on the Meek's Creek drainage, where they apparently can spawn in the inlet area. I once saw a huge one there but could not get close enough for a cast. Lure and streamer anglers have been very successful for large fish for many years.

In the past Middle Velma was a "put and grow" rainbow fishery with many fish over 15". However, planting of this lake is uncertain in the future, until DFG develops a new Fishing Management Plan, though it was planted in 2007. Wild rainbows are currently found in the Rubicon Lake and River system where they freely breed with the goldens that have descended from Clyde Lake. Rainbows can occasionally be seen in the inlet to Rubicon Lake. They can grow to very large size even at high altitudes as long as the lake has a good food source.

Lake of the Woods also has had very large fish and has plentiful food, but it is not clear if they have survived after planting has declined, although a recent DFG survey suggests some trophy sized specimen have made it. They can either move down a stream or up a stream into a lake where they can forage and put on weight. Lake Taupo in New Zealand is famous for such fish. Rainbows are also found throughout most of the smaller streams in the Desolation. Small fish are in the stream between Upper and Lower Velma Lakes, however, brown trout seem to predominate in the lower reaches of this stream as it passes into Eagle Lake.

Goldens (GT)

A golden trout from the outlet stream of McConnell Lake. The fish took an all-purpose beadhead nymph. Larger fish have existed in the Wilderness but alas, no photos.

The golden is similar to that of a rainbow but has developed an incredible color scheme while living in isolation in some small streams in the southern Sierra. It readily interbreeds with the rainbow and rapidly loses its colors. Apart from the striking colors, usually olive at the back fading to gold at the flanks and crimson on the belly, two identifying features are useful. First, it usually retains parr marks throughout life. Parr marks are large dark blotches, about a dozen or so, along the flanks covering about a quarter to a third of the width of the side. They also have fewer spots on their sides than rainbows, usually not going more than halfway down the side, though the tail is usually full of spots. They can be mistaken for brookies if one sees only white edges on the lower fins.

Recent studies suggest that the fish MAY be able to breed in lakes and certainly I and others have seen them try to do this in Lake Number 3. They have an amazing ability to squeeze their way up very small snow melt streams in the spring. Certainly they can spawn in streams that are the outlets of lakes and work their way back up into the lakes. Their brothers, the rainbows, seem to have mastered this trick in Lake of the Woods.

The best places to find these fish have changed since planting has virtually stopped (used to be Cup and Cathedral Lakes). Now the best places to find them are in McConnell Lake and its outlet stream, where the above fish was caught, and in the Rubicon River below Clyde Lake. They are much easier to catch in streams than in lakes.

Recent angler reports, however, have suggested that McConnell may have suffered a winter freeze and lost its population. DFG reports suggest that the population is still fat and happy. It is a long walk to find out if they are still there, but I am pretty sure they are OK and not threatened in this obscure location. I did not mention this resource in the first edition because I considered it a treasure best kept hidden. The Leland Lakes that used to carry them are also now reported barren because of the frogs. The fish moved downstream from the Leland Lakes to populate McConnell. There is a barrier to prevent them moving back to the Leland Lakes.

Browns (BN)

The warm colors of a Crag Lake brown trout. This one was fooled by a flying ant.

The brown is not native to California, or North American for that matter, but is a European import. Its major characteristic is the brown to olive back with lighter brown on the sides. Its spots are usually larger than any other trout and are brown, black and red. Spots can be surrounded by halos of blue-gray. The adipose fin, the one between the dorsal (top) fin and the tail, usually has an orange border. Lake dwelling browns develop a lighter coloring and may look closely similar to their relative, the Atlantic Salmon. My experience with these fish in several environments is that eventually they take on the color of their environment to a remarkable level.

The above specimen is from Crag Lake, which is notorious for them. Probably the largest specimens are in Heather Lake and their habits are described in detail in reference to that Lake. They are also in Lower Velma Lake where they also grow to large size. Most recently large fish have been taken from Eagle Lake. Eagle Lake, which is only about a mile up the trail from Emerald Bay and one of the most heavily used lakes in the Wilderness. The also exist in the stream down from this lake towards Emerald Bay but are a challenge to fish in that difficult fast and rocky water.

Miscellaneous

At one point Stony Ridge and Gilmore Lakes were planted with lake trout or mackinaw. It is a large char, like the brookie, but with gray color. Its tail is forked unlike the square-tailed brook trout. This is a very unlikely catch, except for certain anglers….. Please look at the last page or two of the book for the section on Gilmore Lake.

There have been some cutthroats planted into a few lakes, e.g. Dicks and Hidden. These basically look like rainbows but have a little red "slash" below the lower jaw. They would be a very unlikely catch in the Desolation currently.

It is possible in the Desolation that some streams will be planted with Lahontan Cutthroats (LCT). These were the original fish of Lake Tahoe and at one point lived in the drainage of Floating Island Lake and many other Tahoe tributaries. They still grow to trophy size in Pyramid Lake in Nevada.

STRATEGY

Whether one spin fishes or fly fishes, understanding which lakes to fish, when to fish the lake and where fish are most likely to be found in a lake are essential. Probably key works on these topics are *Sierra Trout Guide* by Ralph Cutter and *Lake Fishing with a Fly* by Ron Cordes and Randall Kaufman. They make several important points.

Which Lakes to Fish

Let's face it; some lakes clearly have better fisheries than others. One of the purposes of this guide is to help you find the better ones. But, the exact status of these lakes will change and the clever advice one month will be the big mistake the next. So it is wise to have some idea of the factors that go into making an excellent fishery in the Sierra and choosing intelligently regardless of the published wisdom.

Distance from Civilization makes some difference, but in the Desolation, one is never really far from a trailhead. Nonetheless, it is a general rule that on most trails the first lake is hit the hardest. More important perhaps is getting off the trail a bit. Phipps Lake has excellent fishing only a couple hundred yards from the Tahoe-Yosemite Trail. But it is not on the trail. Altitude climbed works against you as the highest lakes often have the smallest food base upon which to build a trout population. Thus few of the higher more desolate lakes are worth fishing.

In general the lower the lake, the better the feed, and the bigger the fish. Clearly, lakes with good weed beds have an excellent potential source of insects. Trout will grow big in other lakes like Heather, which has a sparse weedless alpine character but has large numbers of red-side shiners. Finally, the larger the lake, the larger the food base and the bigger fish can potentially grow.

When to Fish the Lakes

The time of day generally has much less to do with fishing success than one might imagine. Noticeably, on most lakes there is a feeding period just after sunset and just before sunrise. One problem with these periods is that often every fish is feeding, including the runts. It is very difficult to cast to Moby Dick if he is surrounded by a dozen aggressive but small body-guards. It is important to realize that if trout only ate at sunrise and sunset they would starve. They are in a sense always eating. They have to be opportunistic. So do not ignore high noon even for browns. Browns are notoriously nocturnal but I have seen them tearing up the shiner population at high noon at Crag Lake. When hunger strikes, they raid the refrigerator.

More important than what time of day is what time of year. One can look very successful if one is either the first or last angler to a lake during any season. The ideal time to get in is when there is a partial ice covering of the lake. The big problem is that in the spring ice on lakes may melt before snow on trails does, so you cannot get in at the right time. Furthermore, in spring more damage is created to trails and lakesides by trampling the wet ground. The fall may be a better choice as long as it does not snow before mid November. It is very hard to get the timing correct. Chuck Yaeger solved this problem by overflying the Golden Trout Wilderness in an F-16 to check out the lakes before he hit the trails. Most of us do not have that option. A good thing to do is to keep some notes on your maps or guides about the exact days you went where. This is a general guide for next year. The other thing is to carefully consider the orientation of trails. Those with southern exposure clear first. Finding a good lake atop a trail with a southern exposure means early and late season access.

If one does have to fish for one week in mid-August, what's one to do? Probably the most important thing is to be prepared to fish deep. The fish are still there, down where the temperature is comfortable. This does not mean the bottom of the middle of a 100' deep lake. These areas are generally without oxygen and devoid of fish. The fish are 20-30' down in a comfortable stratum and they are located where that stratum hits the submerged shore. They move in and out from there to forage. So in August, don't fish the shallows and don't fish the deeps, fish in between. Finally, you may be wise in mid-summer to go for a lake with rainbows as they still feed in the shallows in summer when the brookies and goldens are hiding.

Reading a Lake

Probably the most important thing to do when one approaches a lake for the first time is to control the impulse to start fishing immediately. Most likely you do not have an unlimited amount of time available. Use it to your maximum advantage. Spend a few seconds trying to figure out where best to spend your efforts. Also, when checking out the lake, stay several feet from shore to prevent being spotted, and use polarized sunglasses to help see the fish.

The inlet stream is usually my first choice for fishing a lake. This area is like an air-conditioned buffet line for the fish. The inlet brings in well-oxygenated water, perhaps cooler in the summer, and usually contains insects. Access may be a problem and this is a big reason to use a float tube. Outlets also may concentrate surface insects but they are generally tougher to fish than inlets. The water may be shallow and lack cover for fish. Outlets usually lack a channel.

Channels may be either old flooded stream-beds or areas that receive high flow during spring run-off. Fish are usually oriented in a channel as in a regular stream, i.e. facing upstream. In the channel one wants to work up stream from a position where it is harder for fish to spot you. If there is not much flow, fish still congregate in channels for cover and coolness in the summer.

Shallows will often hold much food but there may be little cover for fish to hide. These areas are often productive as sunset provides the cover of darkness. A big problem is approaching the fish without causing them to scatter. This may be impossible and one may have to sit and wait until they return. One sure thing is that if there is food there, they will come back. Remain stationary and you just become part of the background, as long as you do not dress like a rock star.

Shoals are shallow areas surrounded by deeper water. If you can find them, they often have fish in the environs. Looking at a lake with polarized sunglasses in the morning before the wind comes up may allow you to see shoals not readily apparent later in the day.

Springs are also wonderful if you can find them. Fish will congregate around them for "air conditioning" during the summer and bait fish also like them. They are at times very hard to find but a few things help such as a sandy bottom or bubbles. In the Sierra there is another type of spring which is really an inlet stream that is flowing subsurface under conditions of reduced flow, i.e. the summer. If there is water flowing out of a lake and there is no obvious inlet, think springs.

Shoreline weeds or sunken weed beds usually offer a good chance to find feeding fish, the problem is the approach. Again the float tube is helpful. Sometimes one can get into position on a point or log that overlooks a weed bed and cast around the edges of the weeds. Drop-offs near weeds, shallows or other obvious feeding areas are worth attention. Fish can stay on the deep side of the drop off and watch for food from a position of safety.

Float Tubes

Now that you have heard a bit about all the places fish hide in a lake, it probably has become clear that you cannot get near most of them without a float tube. Unfortunately they cost a lot and they weight a ton. I have tried thin walled tubes which allegedly you can inflate without a bicycle pump. I also watched one of these disintegrate underneath me in a chilly lake. You do not want to be in the middle of a lake when one of these falls apart. Also, they simply will not last long.

A solid tube weighs a considerable amount but they can easily be placed on a frame pack for hiking in. It is useful to buy a frame extender while adds an extra inverted U shaped bar to the top of the frame. This allows much easier fixation with straps (not the bungee cord type) but ones with real tethers.

I have to say the other advantage of the frame pack is you can carry a fish-finder. Yes I have used them in the Desolation. They do not guarantee you a fish if you see them, but they do guarantee not fishing over water that does not contain fish. Cabella's catalogue has a number of inexpensive models with side-scan sonar and attaching points perfect for tubes.

My friend Doug Kulick of KaneKlassics has developed lake fishing for trout with these devices into a science. He guides Webber Lake, which is north of Tahoe City, and often lands 20-30 fish a day from this private impoundment. He has discovered that the fish in the dog days of summer often congregate at a very specific depth in the lake (optimal oxygenation and temperature) and if you miss that exact level, you are out of luck. Getting 20-30 fish a day requires a lot more that just finding them because you have to get down and of course you have to have the right fly.

One can save space by taking tubes in deflated but then one has to carry a bicycle pump. There is an important trick if one does this, carry a valve remover (they are built into the tops of many caps for covering inflation points). To inflate remove the valve, use lung power to get much of the initial air in, replace the valve, and do the last bit with the pump. Taking the valve out temporarily will speed deflation. The Skillful Tuber by Robert Alley has many useful hints.

Probably the most useful hint that I have learned from Alley is to carry two fly rods. Actually, you can easily identify people who have read the book by two rods they have on their tubes. Ninety percent of the time one will be fishing from the tube with a sinking line, but the ten percent of dry fly action will be missed unless one is prepared. Trying to change a spool in a float tube is a good ten minute operation. By the time it is completed the rising fish are invariably gone. Carrying a dry fly set-up while fishing deep allows you to quickly change gears.

Finally, some of us are simply not going to be physically able to carry a float tube, camping equipment and fishing equipment into the Wilderness. One should not forget that there are packers available who can help. In most areas of the Desolation one can employ a packer to "spot" equipment at a certain site for a modest cost. The tremendous advantage of this is that one can carry more equipment than one might otherwise and it opens the backcountry for those who for various reasons cannot carry a large load. My wife has a bad back and simply cannot carry any load. Having a packer help is better than my trying to carry two loads plus all of my fishing toys. Experienced packers who can help include those of the Camp Richardson Corral (530-541-3113) and Cascade Stables (530-541-2055). You may also get the latest fishing tips from these folks.

TACTICS AND TACKLE

Spin Fishing

A basic issue is whether or not to use bait. On long trips it is virtually impossible to bring any live bait such as worms. Bringing any type of minnow into the backcountry is not only impractical but *severely prohibited*- getting such fish into new lakes may lead to competition for limited food supplies and ultimately hurt the trout. Newer cheese type baits tend to melt and make a mess in the heat of the outdoors. Finally, the major problem with bait is that swallowing it makes releasing the fish virtually impossible. Though you may catch fish with bait, most will be small, and a fatally-wounded 4" trout is not worth much to anyone.

In general, lures are much more effective than bait. Not only will you catch more fish, you will catch the bigger ones and you retain the option of releasing fish. More important than selection of the "hot" lure is bringing a selection of both types and sizes. The old standbys are the Mepps, Castmaster, Rooster Tails etc. If the lure is not working, vary the type, size and speed of retrieval. This is especially true if you see fish follow the lure but not take it. The "dirty little trick" used by my fishing friends who both spin and flyfish is to attach either a small streamer or nymph to the bottom hook of the spinner. The fish that follow a spinner without hitting often will hit the smaller fly at the bottom. A good reference to technique is John W.'s site (http://geocities.com/johnwako@sbcglobal.net).

The big limitation of lures is that they imitate only one type of food source, in general, bait fish. Reading below on flyfishing you will see there are many other types of food available for fish in lakes. But, as we all know, flyfishing can get expensive and takes time to learn. A way to get the advantages of flyfishing with spin tackle is to use clear plastic bubbles with flies. These types of floats provide enough weight to allow you to cast a weightless dry fly. Using models that can be filled with water allow you to present a wet fly. The water in the bulb provides weight to cast, but slowly sinks allowing a proper retrieve of the wet fly.

Finally, the lighter the tackle the better. First of all, you don't break your back hauling it in. Second, in terms of scaring fish, throwing a heavy spinner or weighted bait into a lake is similar to throwing a rock. Third, the heavier equipment requires stronger line which is easier for trout to see. Lastly, fish are more fun to play on light tackle.

Fly Fishing

As with spin gear, the lighter the fly tackle the better. In general, 6 weight rods are getting into overkill and make a delicate presentation more difficult. A 5 weight rod is probably the standard.

Lighter rods may be useful in situations where a delicate presentation is anticipated. Heavier rods, however, may be useful in situations where one expects to need to "punch" a fly into a gale or one needs to present heavier flies such as large streamers. For those who cannot make up their minds there is clearly one solution: bring two rods. A heavier rod is useful for undersea operations, i.e. flinging a sinking line, a heavy streamer and dealing with Moby Dick once he's on. The lighter rod is useful for delicate surface operations. Remember, it's very nice to have two rods on a float tube. Finally, two rods are nice if you happen to break one ten miles from the trailhead.

Lines for fishing in midsummer should include the fast-sinking variety. You will need to get deep. The faster you do this, the more time in the target zone. If you plan to be working mostly in the shallows a sinktip is the order; otherwise you will be dredging the slimy bottom all day. Again it is wise to consider taking more than one type of sinking line. Using a terminal loop system will allow one to change sinking tips. Orvis markets a system to do this including loop attachments for the leader end of the fly line. But this can also be accomplished with homebrewed arrangements which allow you to add sinking tippets to meet specific conditions. There are no fly shops in the middle of the Wilderness, so bring some alternative methods of changing sink rate.

What flies to take? It is very clear that for certain lakes cited, such as Heather, you will be completely naked without streamers, i.e. shiner imitations. The Black Nosed Dace works quite well, though the shiners in the Desolation have a red streak to them. Sizes 8 or 10 are fine. Other streamers also work well and as in the case of the spin fisher, it is best to have a variety of types and sizes. Wooly Buggers also are a requirement for a venture into the Desolation. The color is not as important as is the variety. Those tied with a small amount of tinsel seem to have added value, but do not make the tail too long as you get short strikes (a bite on the fly's tail instead of the hook point). Woolly Buggers imitate a number of different potential food types besides shiners, e.g. leeches and worms. In addition a variety of small scud and damselfly imitations are of use in some lakes, e.g. Cup Lake for scuds and Triangle for damselflies.

Terrestrials are extremely important in the Desolation. Winds from the Central Valley bring in a wide variety of insects. The essentials are the ants, including carpenter ants. After Fourth of July grasshopper imitations are a must. These do not have to be the finely tied (expensive) sort. Reasonable approximations suffice. I also carry a number of ant imitations in various colors and sizes including flying ants..

No book on fishing is complete without "the fly box". Well here is the real thing with a selection of flies from the last trip (I did carry six boxes) but the essentials are: Left top, assortment of nymphs, with the keys ones being various forms of the Copper John, bead-head caddis and smaller trout "junk food", as well as some blood midges. Left middle wooly buggers and damsel nymphs (I tied exact imitations of red-side shiners when I started up there only to find out wooly-buggers did better possible because of the jig action with cone heads). The dries include various forms of the Adams and for purists some callibaetis. The Humpy is used as a float for a dropper of one of the bead-heads. Caddis are essential is various sizes as are, of course, the terrestrials.

It is well beyond the scope of this guide to go into the subtleties of insect hatches in the Desolation's lakes and streams. This topic has been covered in detail in a number of publications, the most relevant of which is Cutter's *Sierra Trout Guide*, which has a convenient chart of the basic hatches to be expected over the season. It is going to be a rare day, however, in the Desolation on which one will see cloud-like mayfly hatches and use many drys. We are primarily talking nymphs here. You may also want to carry some Blood Midge pupas. One does not see many stoneflies, but there are extensive damselfly hatches in some lakes, e.g. Lake of the Woods. The one dry fly that is absolutely essential is the Elk Hair Caddis in sizes 12-18. Another useful dry fly is a Humpy, to which you can attach a dropper bead head nymph (e.g., #16 Pheasant Tail). Finally, an assortment of parachute Adams would cover additional unpredictable situations.

Cordes and Kaufmann's work is exhaustive on the use of nymphs in a lake, but, to get started a good rule is that if you think you are doing a slow retrieve, cut your speed in half. In general you are trying to imitate an emerging larval form that starts at the bottom of the lake and rises to the top. So you will allow your offering to sink, and then slowly draw it upward. There are untold hundred of variations to this basic idea. One exception would be the midge pupa which is fished in the film at the surface and allowed to drift. Expect takes to be soft, and leaders must be fine, e.g. 6X. Setting the hook must be an exercise in delicacy, but you will be getting fish on with nymphs. Getting the fish on the reel fast, a light drag, and keeping your hands off the line, spool and handles, will help landing the fish. Remember, these are basically small fish and one does not have to horse them around to land them.

WILDERNESS PERMITS & ETHICS

Regulations of the Wilderness

When I first started going into the backcountry in the 1960s, regulations were rare. They still are, despite over 200,000 visitor days spent in the Desolation each year. The permit system simply insures that you are less likely to see campers when you stay overnight. It also provides the Forest Service with data on use patterns. Day permits are available at most trailheads but overnight permits must be obtained from a ranger station. The two most convenient are on Highway 50 near Placerville (530-622-5061) and in South Lake Tahoe (530-573-2600). If you are planning to stay overnight, call ahead of time and determine the best way to get a permit for your trip.

You simply must have one of these permits. Not having one virtually insures you will run into a backcountry ranger who at best will send you back to the trailhead and at worst will write you a ticket (yes, a $$#@%!!$$ ticket!) and then send you back to the trailhead. Another potential high point of your trip would be to have the same ranger check you for a fishing license which you "forgot". A final boost for your trip would be for that ranger to find you next to an illegal campfire. Gas stoves are OK in the Wilderness (with a fire permit), but please familiarize yourself with the rules on fires before you leave. The reason fires are now outlawed was that the rangers were spending an incredible amount of time cleaning fire pits that campers thought of as garbage disposals and foot deep layers would accumulate in one season. All these regulations are described in detail on the back of the Forest Service map of the area that is available at the ranger stations.

Now, there are some of us who react unfavorably to regulations, permits, and the like. I have to admit there was a lot to be said for the "good old days," but most can live with regulations when they understand the rationale. When entering The Desolation for the first time I am sure many are struck by issues of how to preserve it. Learning how to preserve the wilderness requires knowledge of regulations but what is more important is making the ethical decision to follow the rules and to go beyond them. Just following the permit law may prevent a ticket, but in the long run the Wilderness will still suffer under the relentless pressure of visitors. There are many suggestions for good backcountry practice that require some effort, but if we follow this suggestion we take a step to use the area while preserving it. Below are listed a few such suggestions and their reasoning.

There are several suggestions for good backcountry practice upon which many of us agree (see the work by Cole for a solid review). First of all, how do we prevent the proliferation of unsightly campsites? We should stick to the established campsites at most lakes. The lakes that get any use already have multiple campsites. These spots have clearly been used for decades and look like it. There is little point in trying to establish a new campsite and destroy more of the environment. Usually the sites that have been established are the best anyway. Paradoxically, it may be better to use a virgin campsite rather than one only slightly used. Your using that slightly used campsite will lead to its further downfall. If you are clever about using a virgin site, no one will ever see that it has been used before. Second, regarding trails, like campsites, it's generally best to stick to established trails- the alternative is usually lost time. On established trails please stay in single file to prevent creation of meandering systems of "braided" trails. If you have to go cross-country, do not travel in single file- spread out. This prevents the establishment of new trails and the destruction of untouched lands. Third, we must carry out anything we bring in. One related sin anglers often commit is to throw fish viscera into lakes. These cold waters slow decay and the unsightly leftovers may often be seen a month after the fact. You don't have to carry them out! Better to scatter the viscera on land where they more quickly decay. Fourth, choose clothing and equipment that blends into your surroundings so that you will be less obvious to others seeking solitude- both other campers and fish! Along these lines also try to choose a campsite that is not obviously seen. Fifth, for several easily imagined reasons, one should camp at least 100' from the side of a lake or stream. Finally, there are a number of ethical issues related to fishing.

Fishing Ethics

Catch and release fishing should clearly be practiced where there are limited resources. About 60% of the lakes in the Desolation support brook trout, which naturally reproduce. It is very hard to take too many of these from such lakes and in certain cases there is overpopulation, such as Saucer Lake, which results in stunting (big heads, small tails and they look prehistoric). Yet, this is no reason for taking more than one can eat, particularly of the larger fish. Leaving a few will allow them to grow and get to the size many of us would really appreciate catching. This is particularly important for the 10% or so of lakes in which there are reproducing browns. These fish can grow to a large size if we let them. Finally, some of the lakes of the Desolation cannot support a fish population without planting since they do not have trout that can reproduce in their waters. An example of this would be the rainbows of Middle Velma Lake. One can argue that you might as well take as many fish as you want from this lake since they are replaced by DFG. Yet, I would still argue that fish should be returned to such lakes to allow them to get to larger size. Why not share the trophy? At the time of this writing it is not clear if this lake will be restocked.

Releasing fish is difficult when using bait, especially with small fish. Fly anglers have learned that barbless hooks or hooks on which the barb has been crimped down actually hold better than barbed hooks in most situations. The reason for this is that the smaller diameter of the hook point bites deeper and cleaner. Many fish caught with barbed hooks get off simply because the barb only allows the hook to penetrate to its barbed tip. As long as moderate tension is kept on the line, a fish will not get off a barbless hook, unless he can swim backwards. Releasing the fish itself should be accomplished with wet hands firmly gripping just above the tail and not crushing the fish's internal organs. Gently cradle the upper body while keeping your fingers out of the gills. Some fish may need to be helped in the water before they can swim off safely. Don't allow them to fall over upside down- they may never right themselves. Hold them upright, moving them gently so that water moves through the gills. If you want to take a picture, keep the fish in the water until it is set up and only raise the fish out briefly, or better yet shoot the picture with the fish in the water (a polarizing filter helps in this case).

Finally, we cannot take trout of any source in these lakes for granted. It is important to know that many argue that it is unethical to plant "wilderness areas" at all, or even to foster wild trout propagation in any of these lakes or streams. It is essential to realize that trout will eat indigenous amphibians such as the frogs, which are an officially threatened species. If the situation with the frogs becomes worse, so will the fishing, because even more severe measures will be taken (kiss even more lakes good-by). USFS and DFG are trying to find a compromise that allows both fish and frogs to live together. Make your view known to CalTrout, state and federal managers, and become an advocate for the wise balanced use of the Wilderness!

Spawning male brookies fight for the attention of the female at Azure Lake

SECTION 1: ECHO LAKES

Triangle Lake

The Echo Lakes are outside the Wilderness proper but the entrance road to the Lakes from Highway 50 provides easy access to the backcountry. The real claim to fame of this access is that it starts at over 7400' so that there is little need to gain more altitude. This entrance is made even further attractive by the Pacific Crest Trail along the north shore of the Echo Lakes that due to its overdone construction, has been described as the Santa Monica Freeway of the High Sierra. There is also a pleasant lodge at the start of the trail (Echo Chalet). Finally, to attract even more visitors, there is a water taxi running from the end of the road about 2-3 miles to the end of the upper lake. Thus using this entrance one gets a running start at getting into the Sierra. This fact has not been missed by the hiker and angler and the area is heavily infested with both. Nonetheless, there are interesting lakes in this area which escape the masses as soon as one steps a few hundred yards off the main trails. I find the historic cabins you see at this entrance fascinating.

TRIANGLE LAKE

The easy way to get to Triangle Lake is clearly the Pacific Coast Trail from Echo Lakes, which makes for a very pleasant day hike with little altitude gain. There is also access from the Fallen Leak Lake area via a trail that departs the road just before Lily Lake. This hike is a death march and not to be recommended unless one is marooned at Fallen Leaf Lake (the Stanford Camp) for longer than a week and desperately seeking some fishing. This lake has been stocked with both rainbows and brookies, though it has only received rainbows since 1970. They grow rapidly. Maximum size is about 12-14". I have never caught a brookie here.

Unfortunately for spin anglers the Lake is weedy. One probably could stock a sporting goods store with the snagged lures on the bottom. There is also a large log right in the middle- seen from the hills on a calm day. Fly fishers should strongly consider a float tube, as there is very little backcasting room. The lake is small enough that roll casts can get a long way

15

proportionately into the lake, but a tube is still best. There is one area that supports full fly casts near the point where the trail meets the lake. Do not visit here without damselfly nymphs and adults.

In the fall of 1994 I took a long one-day hike up to Triangle Lake from Lily Lake, and then continued on with help from Wood's Guide cross-country to Heather Lake. Triangle had lots of very pretty Eagle Lake put and grow rainbows. It used to get busy there at times and people should know how to get to Lost Lake (you need a map – it's a well-named lake). The best way is described in Wood's old guide: just when the trail to triangle makes its final descent to the lake, do not descend but follow the granite over to your left. Taking the "Sierra Sidewalk" gets you there easily with a map as long as you pretty much do not change altitude. Going down to Triangle and up the outlet of Lost Lake is much harder. In any case, Lost has many brookies that need culling so that we get some up to size. It has also gotten golden plants but I have never seen one there and they are unlikely to have survived. I repeated this hike in July 2008 and found no fish in Triangle, but lots of brookies in Lost. It is expected that this Lake will be planted again when DFG makes its final plans known (stay tuned).

LOST LAKE

This lake can be part of a trip to Triangle. A topo is necessary to find it, though it is close by. The easiest way to find it is suggested by Wood: from the point on the Triangle Lake Trail that you first see Triangle Lake turn left and contour over (i.e. move left and do not change altitude) and the lake is within a quarter mile. Alternatively one can see the course of the Lost Lake outlet stream from Triangle Lake (a line of trees) and work your way over. Both these routes are off-trail and can easily lead to a broken ankle for the unfamiliar. Some caution is warranted.

This is another brook trout stronghold, which used to receive regular feedings of golden fingerlings, care of DFG. The lake has a good food supply of brookies and the fish are nicely developed. I have yet to catch a golden here. One might find out if they exist in the spring if they go through the motions of spawning in the small inlet stream.

This lake is small and shallow in most parts, except very conveniently right in front of a large boulder at the nearest point to the Triangle Lake Trail. Casting from this area with fly or spin gear is feasible and it provides an excellent picnic spot. These fish are rather smart (for brookies) and hug the bank where it is hard to flycast and impossible to spin cast.

CUP LAKE

This lonely lake in the past offered the best chance for the novice to catch a moderate size golden trout in the Wilderness. One look at a topo map will show why: it is virtually unvisited. Although it is located only 1.5 miles or so from either Upper Echo Lake or Highway 50 below Phillips (Pow Wow), it is at the 8600' level of a very steep mountain. Access can be attempted from Highway 50 up 1700' of scree (rock) slopes. One stays to the east of a small spur. This route is only for those familiar with navigating loose rock. The approach from Echo Lakes is more civilized so long as one can get the water taxi to drop you at Dartmouth Cove. From here a trail leads to Saucer Lake. One starts this climb at 7400' which is 600' higher than the Route 50 approach. One climbs from Saucer Lake to a ridge to its south then west to overlook and descend to Cup. The problem with this approach is the descent, which again is over scree, and the depressing fact that one has to go back up to regain

Arrival at Lost Lake from Triangle Lake

the ridge after leaving Cup. A final issue is that unless you make careful arrangements you will find no water taxi waiting for you when you return to Dartmouth Cove. This leads to a long walk around Echo to return to your car. In either case, getting to Cup is an adventure, but one that can be accomplished in a single day.

Cup Lake had been air-stocked with goldens since the 1960s. I have taken fish up to 14" from here. They seem to have the unusual food source of some fresh water shrimp. The flesh of these fish is bright red, quite different from that of other lakes. The taste is exotic. According to a 2003 DFG survey this lake filled with brookies after air planting stopped. A small air plant of goldens occurred in 2007 and is projected to occur annually. Reports on this lake would be appreciated.

The most important point of strategy on this lake is to arrive at the right season, either early spring or late fall. The fish are clearly feeding at these times and are near the surface and in the shallows. In the summer the fish scatter and are in deeper water, hence are virtually inaccessible. The big problem with selecting the spring and fall seasons to visit is the unpredictability of the weather. I have found that the Lake starts to freeze over about November 10th. This, however, will vary from year to year. A wild card in visiting the Lake is snow. Any appreciable snowfall makes the trip impossible since one cannot move safely over boulder fields half covered with snow. Light snow burns off on the south-facing slope above Highway 50, so this really is the mostly likely approach. My experience with the spring is that by the time the snow melts, so has the ice on the Lake, and it is not worth the trip.

SAUCER LAKE

The access to this Lake has already been described in reference to a trip to Cup. This Lake in and of itself is not worth the effort of the climb. It almost led to a divorce in my family. However, if you poop out on the way to Cup, at least there are some fish to be had at Saucer. I would not like to make the approach early in the season when the north facing trail is likely to be very wet, if passable at all.

Goldens have been stocked in this lake since the 60s. There is a surviving population of brookies. The brookies are perhaps the best (worst) example of stunted trout I have seen in Desolation. Apparently the meals are few and far between here and anglers do not cull the population. If you do fish this lake, take a few. Perhaps in their new Plan, DFG can clean out this small lake and put something a bit more interesting into it, such as goldens.

TAMARACK LAKE

This name is really a misnomer, as the true Tamarack pine (Larix or Eastern Larch) does not live in California. Often the lodgepole (Pinus contorta) is referred to as a tamarack pine and this is probably the source of the name. The lake is easy to reach from the Pacific Crest Trail. Unfortunately, since it is so easy to reach, the shore-line has been heavily overused at the point where the trail meets the lake. For that reason alone I put this lake low on my list of attractions. There are, however, other good campsites around the lake. This is a brook trout fishery and the best hope in this lake is the inlet area, though access is easy along most of the shoreline and there is room for flyfishing along the southwest shore. A 2008 survey showed no fish and this is a likely site for frog habitat.

RALSTON LAKE

Ralston Lake is named after William Chapman Ralston, a prominent financier of gold-rush days. It is right next to Tamarack Lake and is a pleasant visual alternative, especially given its striking alpine setting. This lake has received both brookies and rainbows and they get to moderate size. This is a large lake with deep cuts near shore. A float tube would be extremely useful for cruising the edge. A particularly interesting spot is just across the stream outlet dam where a bluff enters the water.

I met the person who constructed this dam, Haven Jorgensen, who was a member of the Mount Ralston Fish Planting Club (MRFPC). He has now passed away. This dam was the last constructed in the area and is in some disrepair due to Jorgy's attempt to use less mortar between the stones to give the dam a more natural appearance. This dam provides enough flow into Echo Lakes to provide spawning for its residents. Jorgy noted that the clever angler can find trout all along this stream and in particular along the small stretch down to Cagwin Lake.

CAGWIN LAKE

Cagwin is just downstream from Ralston and is named after the "Hermit of the Lake" Hamden "El Dorado" Cagwin a hunter and fisherman who settled on Lower Echo Lake in 1896. The "Hermit" was an accomplished snowshoer and carried the mail from Strawberry to Carson City. This smallish lake has received primarily rainbows but you can bet there are also brookies from upstream. Much of the Lake is shallow and not prime territory except for the southwest rocky shore where there are deeper areas near drop-offs. Tamarack, Ralston and Cagwin may become fishless in the latest frog sanctuary proposal.

SECTION 2: DESOLATION VALLEY

The "Japanese Garden"

The Desolation Wilderness, created in 1966, takes its name from this valley. Originally it was called the "Devil's Valley" in the 1880s. Conservation of the area began in 1910 with the creation of the El Dorado National Forest, followed by designation of the Desolation Valley Wild Area in 1931. Access to this area is either up the Horsetail Falls Trail from Twin Bridges on Highway 50 or across from Lake of the Woods and the Echo Lake area. Going up the Horsetail Falls Trail with a full pack is an experience not likely to be repeated. In crucial areas it is no more than a rocky slope with cairns (stone piles which serve as trail markers and sometimes also called "ducks"). If you really want to visit this area, the side-door from Echo Lakes, though less direct, is much easier hiking with a full pack.

Although there are a number of unique lakes in this area, one soon finds oneself wandering from tarn to tarn without much caring which is which due to the spectacular scenery. The area is really the heart and soul of the Desolation. It is wide-open, full of small lakes, glacier polished granite and peaks. It is an area to explore without a preplanned itinerary.

AVALANCHE LAKE

Really a wide spot in Pyramid Creek just above the falls, it serves as a rest stop for those who have survived the climb up the trail or as pause for reflection for those concerned about breaking a leg on the way down. This lake has received mostly rainbows, but the area above is teeming with brookies. Rainbows love fast water and there is fast water here. In fact, fish really liking such water just have to head downstream for the fast water ride of their lives. I would not go wading about anywhere near the falls. One can sometimes see fish in the current within casting distance of the shore. We do not know if the rainbows have reproduced in the wild here.

In this "lake" one fishes where there is the most current. Flyfishing is possible both with drys into the current or nymphs on a strike indicator or a "dropper". The "dropper" technique allows one to fish a dry on top and a nymph below. There are several ways to attach the nymph. I prefer to tie an additional blood knot near the end of my tippet leaving extra line on the tags. This allows you to attach two flies: you can either attach the dry on top which allows the wet to drop to the same depth as the tag you have left, or you can attach the wet on top which allows the wet fly to remain near the surface in the "film".

PITT LAKE

This is the next stop up the trail from Avalanche Lake. There are a number of little lakelets in this area and the geography is confusing. Suffice it to say all the lakelets are all part of the same complex and most have fish visible to the casual observer. Here, stealth is critical to fishing success. You will usually see the fish before you cast. Light equipment and a delicate presentation are essential both for fly and spin fishing alike. Pitt, like Avalanche, has a current. A good place to find brookies is where the lake narrows. Fish

congregate here as in a feeding lane in a stream. Fish may also be found next to the extensive weedbeds and in Pyramid Creek above the lake.

ROPI, TOEM, OSMA, GEFO LAKES

Many of the lakes of this area were unnamed when the Mount Ralston Fish Planting Club (MRFPC) began its work in the 1920s. The members gave the lake names an "Indian" flavor by using the first two or three letters of their first and last names, thus Ropi is from ROss PIerce. This operation worked better with some names than others. Toem Lake was named after Tom Emery of the MRFPC; Gefo after George Foss.

These lakes form a chain to the west above Ropi and provide pleasant brook trout fisheries. The highest of the chain, Gefo, though very attractive, is shallow and subject to winter-kill. This is the death of fish during the winter, not due to freezing, but deoxygenation of the water. My understanding is that this lake will appropriately be left to the frogs. Toem usually has an excellent population regardless of the winter. It is only a few feet higher than Ropi and offers some good spots for flycasting. In Ropi, one should particularly check the well-oxygenated inlet area. Due

The inlet to Pitt Lake... notice the riffle where the water enters.

Gefo Lake on a calm day.

to the interconnections of these lakes with the following it is unlikely that fish could be eliminated. It will be interesting to see what type of fishery develops.

PYRAMID AND WACA LAKES

These lakes also drain into Ropi, but from the northwest. Access is via the Ropi-Toem-Gefo chain or from Lake Aloha. Named after Walter Campbell of the MRFPC, Waca Lake and Pyramid Lake are currently fishless. Pyramid Lake should not be confused with the Pyramid Peak Lakes that are on the other side of Pyramid Peak but are also barren of fish.

In the 1993 edition I stated: "Many of the tarns in the area are full of frogs and tadpoles. Green woolly buggers are effective in the two main lakes." It turns out fifteen years later that these areas will be frog refugia, assuming the fish really can be removed. How things change. Please see the portrait of some particularly attractive Mountain Yellow-Legged Frogs in Section 4. They are primarily found on the western side of the Desolation. In other words, Sections 2-4 are Frog Country. These two lakes may have the best population in the Wilderness, so worth a visit if you want to see the critters.

DESOLATION, CHAIN, CHANNEL AND AMERICAN LAKES

This officially-named Chain of Lakes is to the northeast of Ropi and is, as with the other chains of lakes, brookie fisheries. There have been plantings of rainbows sporadically in these areas, so one may be surprised. This particular area is one of the most pleasant places in the Wilderness to wander about fishing. There are many idyllic pools and channels all with a certain number of fish. The biggest problem is getting lost or on the wrong side of a channel across from where one would like to be. But one should not be in a rush to pass through. The stream into American Lake deserves particular attention, not right where it enters the lake, but a bit further into the lake where it broadens and deepens. This is a feeding line with good shelter, i.e. a prime lie. Part of this area, between Chain (unnamed on the map) and Channel, resembles a formal Japanese Garden and was so named by the Echo Lake cabin owners. Fish may be found throughout the area both in streams and lakes. The bottom lake, Desolation, is easily linked to Lake of the Woods cross-country, or from Ropi, down Pyramid Creek.

LAKE OF THE WOODS

This is an extremely productive lake that could assure great fishing if it were not so close to civilization. Its shores are highly eroded from years of use by travelers, primarily from the Echo Lakes basin, the main access point to the rest of the lakes described in this section. Brookies have done better in here than rainbows as plants but both develop to good size due to the extensive feed available. There are wide weed beds along the shores that provide both food and cover for the fish. Even in the middle of summer rainbows venture close to shore to feed, and they can be of size. A float tube is again very helpful to attain deeper water and to fish back towards the weed beds.

Here is a quote from "streamkeeper" Greg Puccioni who made a heroic day hike into the lake. Sounds like it was worth it:

> - made a day hike into Lake of the Woods from Twin Bridges this past weekend. Brought along my fishing gear for the heck of it. First time I had been to the lake. Got one bite, and it

was a great fish. Can't say I fully landed it, as it snapped my line just a foot from shore b/c I didn't have my net (never again!) with me (4 lb. test not strong enough to "guide it in" even though it was pretty tired). I am just curious about the overall fishing at this lake. This Rainbow had to be 17-18" and it was a relatively fat fish. By far the largest fish I have hooked in the desolation area. No other bites or sightings, although I hooked the fish in the dead middle of the afternoon (2 o'clock)... How big do the Rainbows get in this or any other lake in Desolation? I didn't think they got that big...

The answer to the question of how big they get is interesting. My favorite lake in the Emigrant Wilderness is Emigrant Meadow. This lake, with the same sort of weedbeds as Lake of the Woods, and at 9000', sports well-documented rainbows over 20". It's a good thing the lake is 10 miles from Kennedy Meadows Pack Station (the best way in is on a horse). Lake of the Woods is a lot closer, but I would not go up the Falls, rather, would take the water taxi.....

Lake of the Woods at Ice-Out, just a little too early for fishing.

21

Lake of the Woods during the summer.

FRATA LAKE

Named after Frank Talbot of the MRFPC, this lake provides a marginal brookie fishery, is shallow, and subject to winter-kill. It is overshadowed by its big neighbor described above. As Wood said, this lake is better for swimming than fishing.

LAKE LUCILLE AND LAKE MARGERY

Lake Lucille is named after Lucille Meredith, a banker's wife of the early 1900s. These two shallow lakes are brookie fisheries. They are hit hard due to their proximity to the Pacific Crest Trail and are not too far from Lake of the Woods. Less often used (with good reason) is the small trail that leads down (or up) to Grass Lake and Fallen Leaf Lake. These lakes are not worth the hike from Fallen Leaf. If you come over here cross-country from Lost Lake it is easy to miss the trail from Grass Lake because it is so overgrown.

If one really needs to fish one or the other, Lucille is superior. A recent report suggests the fishing has picked up in Lucille with hoppers, ants (sunken under indicators and floating) and small nymphs. I picked up a nice brookie here in 2008 with a Copper John. There were several spin fishermen at the lake who reported good success.

The Copper John in lakes is fished a bit like a spinner, that is it is cast into likely water and then slowly and irregularly retrieved. The Copper John comes in three flavors: original (copper), red and green. All the red ones in my fly boxes are gone, if that tells you anything. These are of the same size as is used for nymphing for steelhead on the Trinity River, that is, large, # 12 and # 14. The weight of the fly obviates need for additional split-shot in casting. These larger versions also must to a certain extent mimic damselfly nymphs. I have a collection of damsel nymphs and it appears that the smallest most sparsely dressed flies do the best.

They are often fished with a sinking tip line, however, this is not a necessity in the Desolation. If you read the section of Half Moon Lake you will see an angler report on how the fish will sit inches from the shore. One of the tricks to getting these wary feeders to strike is to somehow place the fly between them and the shore. They seem to cue to insect activity right on the shoreline.

Lake Lucille where the trail from Grass Lake arrives.

Lake Aloha from the Pacific Crest Trail

LAKE ALOHA

The origin of this lake's name is unclear since it is anything but a tropical setting. [Craig Fusaro from CalTrout who helped edit this suggested there might be an AL O'HARA in the MRFPC history somewhere]. On a map this is the largest appearing lake in the Desolation, but it does not hold a huge amount of water. It was enlarged by a PG&E dam that allows the water to run out during the summer for the power company's purposes. Thus what may be an alpine landscape in spring turns to a lunar landscape by fall. These shifts in depth do not do the fishing any good. It has received extensive plants of both brookies and rainbows in the past and now has a good brookie population.

One trick to the lake is to wait to fish it until the fall when the water level drops and the fish are more concentrated. Furthermore, one should examine the seldom-visited rocky shoreline past the trail to Mosquito Pass. The side of the lake next to the Pacific Crest Trail is very heavily used and visited by day hikers using the water taxi from the Echo Lakes.

LAKE LE CONTE

This granite-bound lake above the inlet to Heather Lake is named after Professor Joseph Le Conte (1823-1901) a geologist who wrote extensively about glaciation in the High Sierra. The shore and setting demonstrate this glaciation and provide a scenic camping site, much more isolated than the sites commonly used next to Lake Aloha. This lake has received both rainbows and brookies. These fish have not grown to any size, but they were readily available over the years. In 1996 DFG looked into LeConte and found medium sized brookies and rainbows. It is not clear if the rainbows can survive without planting. The outlet stream is most likely to be a one-way street down to Heather Lake, where as far as I know rainbows have never been seen. I have not seen any angler reports on the brookie population but DFG sees the population in decline.

JABU LAKE

Named after Jack Butler of the MRFPC, this lake provides an incredible view of the Fallen Leaf area from its outlet stream. It has only been stocked with goldens. I was never able to catch a fish here during the 1990s, but reports indicated that they existed but did not grow large. I suspect that I have arrived at the wrong season. According to DFG in 1996, despite my lack of success there in the past, the lake still had medium-sized goldens. It is not clear than any could have survived over the years. This lake does provide a campsite slightly off the beaten path. Lucille, Margery and Jabu may become fishless in the latest frog proposal (http://www.fs.fed.us/r5/ltbmu/projects).

SECTION 3: WRIGHT'S LAKE

They do get this big in "Section 3"... reel is 3" across

The area around Wright's Lake receives much use. The blacktop road in from Highway 50 brings many vacationers each year, yet there are a few places rarely visited in this area that afford some fine fishing. The road to Wright's Lake also affords access to the Barrett Lake jeep trail and more fishing in a different drainage, with some of the biggest brookies in the Desolation.

LYONS LAKE

The Lyon's Lake trail is not heavily used, but traverses some very pleasant forest and the stream which parallels the trail occasionally has the odd fish. Lyon's Lake is itself the largest lake on the trail and a fine goal for this 5 mile walk. The lake is in a granitic valley and has a good population of resident brookies. The fish do get large here but are not as easily caught as in Lake Sylvia. A prime spot for fishing is around the inlet stream, but this is best reached by float tube due to bushes. Other good areas include the boulder fields that enter the water next to the inlet stream. One can cast to the inlet area from rocks to either side, but the casts are long. There are also small fish that respond to a fly in the outlet stream and its lakelet. In 2003 there was a report from John Wakabayashi that Lyons Lake had nice brookies to 14".

LAKE SYLVIA

This lake is less used than Lyon's Lake but provides an extensive brookie fishery. The fish are on the verge of overpopulation but are not yet stunted. One can easily camp at either lake and fish both. Getting to this lake requires less altitude gain than getting to Lyon's Lake but the setting, though quite nice, is not as spectacular. The inlet stream is a good spot but there are fish throughout the lake.

This lake does provide probably the shortest access point for those who want to try to climb Pyramid Peak, and thus becomes an excellent spot for parties including alpinists who don't fish. The view from the top of the Peak is unbelievable with the whole Wilderness spread out below.

GROUSE LAKE

The next trail in the Wright's Lake area leads from Wright's Lake to the east. It is heavily used but there are fish, brookies, especially, near the inlet stream. This may be planted with goldens in the future. One alternative to the heavily used area of Grouse Lake is Secret Lake which is directly south and also has brookies. This requires a cross-country jaunt.

Tyler grave by Tom Hoffman: Don't forget the parka.

HEMLOCK LAKE

This small lake is named after the stand of mountain hemlock on the south shore. This is a pleasant small lake with a good resident population of small brookies. Casting is at times a problem due to the brushy shore.

SMITH LAKE

The final destination of this trail at 8700' is alpine Smith Lake. This lake is larger than the two one passes on the way up and offers the most attractive campsites. It is heavily populated with brookies. According to Wood, alpinists may also be able to find a way to Lyon's Lake from here.

TWIN LAKE

The trail to Twin and Island Lakes branches off at a lower altitude from the Smith Lake trail and appears to get more use. I once saw a grandfather taking his grandchildren up here on the backs of some llamas. There are, however, a few spots near here that may be a bit underused such as the outlet steam from Island Lake. This goes into a little lakelet via some falls. Fish love this oxygenated water especially in high summer. Boomerang Lake on the way to Island Lake also allegedly contains brookies as may Umpa Lake to the northwest. So there are possibilities for expeditions to hidden places even in this overused basin.

ISLAND LAKES

These Lakes were once stocked with goldens but the resident brookies made short work of them and the planting was eventually stopped. This is a barren but striking alpine basin with a reasonable fishery. In his guide Robert Wood, describes a cross-country route to Clyde Lake starting in this cirque. Looking at the cliff above the Lake, this adventure does not appeal to me.

BARRETT LAKE

The hiker (or jeeper) can reach Barrett Lake via the Barrett Lake jeep trail leaving from Dark Lake in the Wright's Lake area. This trail is virtually unused in early season before it is open to jeeps. Barrett Lake is outside the Wilderness but this lake and its outlet stream provide good brook trout fishing.

LAWRENCE LAKE

The first stop out of Barrett Lake is Lawrence Lake. This is a fine brookie fishery with fish of all sizes in quantity. They will congregate at the inlet stream from Top Lake. Lost or "Gem" Lake directly west of Lawrence Lake just inside the Wilderness also provides brookie fishing off the beaten path. Lake Number 9, due east, is barren.

TOP LAKE

A fairly obvious trail leads from Lawrence up to Top Lake. This lake received golden plants in the 1990s but has always had a number of large brookies that appear to have used the goldens as a vitamin supplement. There are fewer fish here than at Lawrence but there are some large (read smart) ones. This lake provides spectacular camp-sites with views overlooking the Sacramento area. There is plenty of casting room for fly fishers and nymphs work well.

According to a 1990s DFG survey the goldens did survive. I have been pretty skeptical of this in the past, but I guess they have found them alive there. In my recollection of the lake there is a granite shoulder that provides casting access to its lower portion where the large brookies are. On calm days in early and late season they will be seen leisurely taking midges.

LAKE NUMBER 5

The Red Peak Trail out of Barrett Lake leads to this swampy lake. It has a marginal brookie population and a massive mosquito population. Circa 1995 DFG found some 2 lb. brookies in Lake No. 5. I haven't gotten one yet. Also, there is a lake that had some "inadvertent"

A sinister Maude Lake as a storm rolls in.

DFG plants 1.5 miles due west of Onion Flat (Rubicon Reservoir) and almost 2.0 miles NNE of Highland Lake. This lake will not be planted again, but on my last journey up there I heard reports of some 16 year old anglers that they caught "lots of 15" rainbows" there. But can they reproduce?

LAKE NUMBER 3

One lake I kept off the map in the original edition is probably safe to publicize -- Lake No. 3. It turns out that the State Trout (the Golden) can reproduce in the smallest of inlet or outlet streams. Before I published the first edition of the guide in 1993 I visited this lake during some drought years in early spring when rainbows and goldens spawn. Well, there were a number of spawners in the outlet as well as in little snowmelt streams. If you go downstream from the lake there are a lot of small fish. This stream goes for miles through desolate country and probably has fish in pools. Now, one other thing that is interesting about this lake is that according to Wood (p. 148) there is a cross-country route across the saddle between Red and Silver Peaks that links Lake No. 3 with the Leland Lakes (more goldens in the time of 1993 but I believe they have all been gill netted out to provide room for frogs). This lake has received plants in 2003 and 2007.

TYLER LAKE

The Rockbound Pass trail receives heavy use linking Wright's Lake and Rockbound Valley. The Tyler Lake offshoot is relatively less used and provides some interesting opportunities. On the way up watch at about the 7860' level for the Tyler's grave lateral trail. This short trail is marked with an enameled sign which is easy to miss on the way up the trail but easier to see while descending. Tyler was a ranch hand who froze to death in an early season storm near the lake that bears his name. His grave is in a quiet dell about 100 yards off the main trail with a white marble military headstone. It is one of those places that gives the Wilderness some of its character. In any case, the lake itself is well supplied with goldens thanks to some recent plants.

GERTRUDE LAKE

This pleasant small lake slightly below Tyler was stocked with goldens. They are currently gone. One may want to walk down the outlet stream to look for fish. This is apparently frog-habitat, so say hello if you see one. Reports on this area would be appreciated.

MAUD LAKE

It is hard to believe that one might find good fishing in this lake right on the autobahn between Wright's Lake and Rockbound Valley. Nonetheless, there are fish in the lake and, of interest to fly fishers, also in the outlet and inlet streams. Using a stealthy approach one will find large fish, mostly brookies, hidden in undercuts of the inlet stream. These fish are not easy to approach but provide an insight to the size of fish that can live even in an overused lake like Maud. There are also fish in the outlet stream and in its lower reaches (the Jones Fork of Silver Creek reached from the Barrett Lake jeep trail) that appear to be mostly wild rainbows.

SECTION 4: ROCKBOUND VALLEY

Rubicon River (Rockbound) Valley with Clyde Lake at its head.

There are several obvious access routes into this area. Luckily for camping solitude, most of the routes involve such distance as to make day trips impossible.

ROCKBOUND LAKE

This lake's name dates to the last century, with Rockbound Pass dating to 1915. The Pass was designed as an emergency escape route for cattle in the event of an early snow. Access to this area is usually achieved via the jeep trail to Buck Island Lake, which is outside the Wilderness boundary. The Rubicon Springs area on this jeep trail receives heavy use, but the old foot trail around the north side of Rockbound Lake and on to Fox Lake is quite unused. Hikers often enter via Loon Lake and the major trail beginning there. This trail is the old construction road for Rubicon Reservoir. There are still fish in the old outlet course to the Rubicon River from Rubicon Reservoir, but this area is a shadow of what it once was before the construction of the reservoir. There are browns, brookies and planted rainbows in this lake as well as possibly some brookies in small, seldom-visited Fox Lake. Fox was barren in a 2003 survey.

RUBICON RESERVOIR

This is a totally artificial addition to the Wilderness which flooded the old Onion Flat area (see old topos). There is no point in recounting the destruction of the Rubicon River as a wild trout stream by this construction in the late 1950s and early 1960s, but suffice it to say that the Rubicon used to have steelhead and was a world famous trout stream. It now runs wild (when there is water) for less than 10 miles into this reservoir. There are browns, brookies and rainbows. The proof that the Rubicon River is still wild is that one will catch rainbow-golden hybrids in it. Even in a dry year they may be found in pools and the fish share some of the characteristics of both rainbow and golden.

CLYDE LAKE

The headwaters of the Rubicon start at Clyde Lake (top of the aerial). This lake was planted with goldens and they stretch their way down the canyon where eventually they intermix with the rainbows moving up from Rubicon Reservoir. The latest DFG surveys show no fish and a healthy population of frogs. Clyde Lake itself has an Arctic feel to it, especially in the spring and fall. It is surrounded by a huge cirque with "interesting" cross-country routes on the rim, well-described in Wood's guide. This Lake is best accessed from Lake Aloha and Mosquito Pass.

I did my own scouting about in the Rubicon River area above the Reservoir in September 1996. Flows were down to a trickle in the stream but it was still quite pretty, especially when it comes over granite slabs in many places. I caught a number of rainbow-golden hybrids up to 12" in the river's pools. The goldens drop down from Clyde Lake and the rainbows move up from the reservoir. I also fished the Reservoir but did not do well. This place is probably better suited for spin equipment. I saw just one large fish in the inlet area-there may be more when flows are higher- a friend went in the following week and the fish was still there and he landed it. In 1996 I said that next time I'm going to bring a small inflatable boat. Never made that trip, but for those of you with an adventurous streak and a good 4X4, look at the Meeks Bay off-road trail (Rubicon) and ask yourself some questions about how to get in here.

I have long supported the use of stream-flow dams at the outlet of such lakes to keep flow up in the streams. This Lake has a very small one, I recall. It might be that without the dam here the fish could spawn in the river and move up to the lake to grow. This may not happen, as it appears that this area may contain frogs. I almost hesitate to include the following information from a "streamkeeper" report from 2000, but it is so hard to get to this area I have little fear the fishing will decline from overuse and I doubt much has changed since 2000.

This streamkeeper, whose e-mail has gone dead, hiked down the Rubicon and fished the meadow stretch at China Camp. At Camper Flat they caught brookies but found golden-rainbow hybrids (if somebody goes in there, please send some photos). The fish were found in slow runs and rocky depressions. The China Camp stretch was reported to be the best area with meandering sections filled with brookies. The fish were caught on a variety of flies including hoppers, wet flies and red leaches. There was an evening hatch.

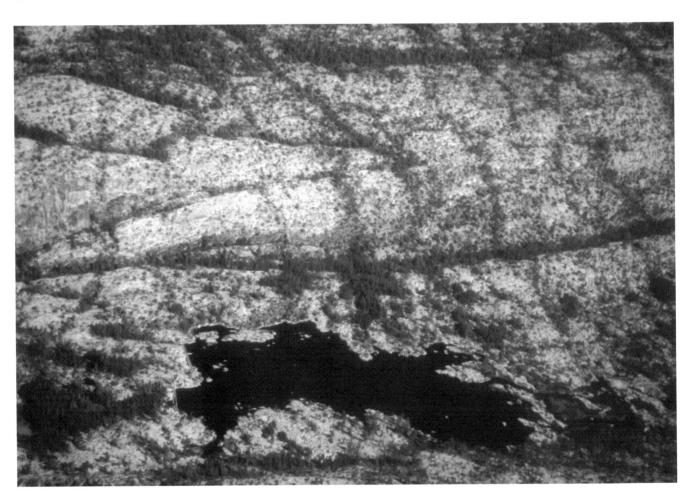

Rubicon Reservoir from the air. On the left (north side) is Fox Lake with the sharp edge of the dams. On the right (south side) you will see the productive inlet area. The mass of granite leads up vaguely towards Richardson Lake. Few people venture here, except for the unique personalities often found in Rubicon Springs.

LAKE DORIS

This lake is actually two closely-attached lakes which are in the high alpine valley on the northeastern side of Rockbound Pass. They were stocked with goldens but have held brookies in the past, and there are probably still some there. Fishing has never been good in this lake due probably to the altitude (8400') and the likelihood that snow may fall heavily on this side of the Pass and lead to winter-kill. Anglers probably should keep on walking past these lakes. This particular lake is far from frog populations so may be a candidate for reintroduction of goldens or rainbows when DFG finishes their Plan for the Wilderness. So stay tuned and this information will be updated on the web as soon as news comes out.

LAKE LOIS

Moving down from Rockbound Pass one next spies Lake Lois. This lake is much larger than its sister Doris and is a brook trout fishery. Camping sites are poor around the lake and it tends to be wind-swept, reducing its popularity with overnighters (who drop down into sheltered Lake Schmidell). But this lack of camping attention may be an advantage to the angler. There are many rocky points off which fish gather and reports have generally been good over the years.

LAKE SCHMIDELL

This is a large, deep lake with an extensive brookie fishery. Fish come in all sizes and are plentiful. Particularly good areas to fish are the hard to reach inlet streams on the southwest corner of the lake. Of high interest to the catch and release fly fisher is the small lakelet just below the outlet dam. This lake is teeming with small trout that take readily to the fly. There is plenty of good casting room and an attractive inlet stream that provides continuous action. In early morning and evening there are rises covering this lake. There have been consistently good reports on this lake over the years.

LELAND LAKES

These lakes were stocked with goldens but the fish did not seem to do well. There are more frogs than fish in the upper lake. The edges of the lakes are shallow in most spots and it is difficult to find fish in midseason. Access to this area is hard in the spring and fall. The shortcut that connects these lakes with Lake Schmidell mentioned by Wood in his guide is not worth the effort considering the good trail between the two areas. A general rule is three miles on a trail moves as quickly as one mile cross-country- and without twisted ankles. My understanding is that this is prime frog territory and that fish in these lakes have been removed.

Rubicon River resident.

McConnell "Lake" natural reproduction of golden trout... including the outlet stream... in 1994... but reports in the 2000s have suggested a reduced and fading population

MCCONNELL LAKE

I guess I can let the story out on this "Lake" now. In the early 1990s it was full of wild golden trout. They went up and downstream from this "lakelet" which is more swamp than lake. But, in 2005 John Wakabayashi found nothing at all here. This is about as far away from anything you can get in the Desolation, but I would like to know if the fish are still there. One trip I plan to take is to revisit Lake Number 3 and try to bushwhack my way over to the McConnell area.

When I fished it for the first edition I brought a set of waders into the lake and was able to wade all over the place on a sandy bottom. It was full of small to medium size goldens, as was the stream down from the Leland Lakes. As one can see from the photo it is virtually impossible to approach from the sides due to the weed population. Casting and retrieving anything either spin or fly in this situation is very difficult. I recall there was one small rocky outcrop that might have offered a possibility.

However, I did see and catch fish in the outlet stream as far down as I could hike. The fish in the outlet stream, as are most goldens, quite naïve. The largest golden I have ever caught was in this stream in a perfect hiding spot next to a large rock. I climbed the rock to get a drag-free drift and slid off when I got the hook up, scratching my new Abel reel. I hung on for dear life and landed him, but alas, no photos.

HIGHLAND LAKE

This lake gets more use than one might imagine from its location. The secret is that many campers and packers go cross-country from a number of starting points including the Tell's Peak Trail and Rubicon Reservoir. The Lake did provide one of the better pure rainbow fisheries in the Wilderness. Fly fishers will be attracted to the outlet stream, which has a number of wild fish in its streambed and lakelets.

Many of the lakelets in this area have had fish in them possibly due to errant DFG air plantings. There have been few recent reports. Most of these smaller lakes were planted with rainbows and it is not at all clear that they could survive without spawning habitat. Many of these lakes are named on DFG charts but they are of no consequence if they are not planted. When they were planted they produced large fish, however, they probably also produced a nightmare for any local frogs and it is likely that this whole area will never see another planted trout. The latest DFG surveys have shown few fish in these areas. The ultimate fate of this lake from a fishery point of view is yet to be determined. Again, stay tuned.

Seldom visited Horseshoe Lake in the northwest corner of the Desolation.

ZITELLA, HORSESHOE AND THE 4-Q'S LAKES

All of these lakes are shallow brook trout fisheries and relatively isolated. I believe Zitella is subject to winter-kill. These swampy areas around the 4-Q lakes are not particularly inviting, especially in early season with wet ground and mosquitoes. Nonetheless, there is food for trout in these lakes and you may be surprised by the size of some of the larger residents. Zitella was fishless in a 2003 survey but Horseshoe had fish. This is Frog Country. Details on their identification and more is found at http://www.mylfrog.info/ run by the Sierra expert, Roland Knapp.

Your new friends, the Mountain Yellow-Legged Frog (MYLF), from CDFG Mitch Lockhart.

SECTION 5: MEEKS CREEK

This popular area receives heavy use. The Tahoe-Yosemite Trail is its thoroughfare and it is built to high standards. This is generally an overnight use area since the first lake is 4.6 miles in with a 1200' elevation gain. Some, however, do hike in for the day to the closest lakes. There are fish in Meeks Creek all along this trail, but fishing is difficult due to heavy undergrowth. Where access is easy, habitat degradation has occurred through heavy human use (waders and swimmers). Getting to the stream in many places requires a considerable effort.

Some interesting information dates from a 1997 DFG/USFS trip into the desolation: "We (Stafford Lehr et al.) surveyed lakes in the Meeks Drainage: Lake Genevieve, Crag Lake, Hidden Lake, Shadow, Stony Ridge, and Rubicon Lake. Genevieve, and Crag had good sized (some in the 14 to 15 inch range) RT's, BN's, and BK's and believe it or not Lahontan Cutthroats (don't know how they got there). Forage is primarily redsides, tui chubs and speckled dace along with the assortment of small caddis and midges. The BN's and RT's are self-sustaining. Hidden had good sized RT's and CT's. Shadow had BK's but not much size. Stony Ridge had good sized LT and RT's (one RT exceeded 3lbs). Forage for the larger fish are the numerous non-game fish mentioned above. Rubicon Lake had the typical assortment of BK's. I recommend for all of the lakes with larger fish that a minnow pattern, sinking line stripped slowly along." A more recent survey found similar results.

The good thing about this drainage is that all the lakes are linked together by streams, so natural

The Tallent Lakes. The Lake in the lower left side below the wing tip is Rubicon, then down the valley to Stony Ridge, Shadow, Hidden, Crag and Genevieve. From the intrepid glider pilot, James D'Andrea

reproduction should be fine. In the past I have fished the lakes from a float tube and gotten a smorgasbord of fish. Who knows what will dominate without planting, but I suspect it will be a combo of BN and BK.

LAKE GENEVIEVE

This lake is the first stop about 4.6 miles up the Tahoe-Yosemite trail from Meeks Bay. Because it is the closest of the Tallent Lakes it receives attention from day-hikers. It is primarily a brook trout fishery with some browns. One really needs a float tube to do this lake justice. The shorelines are shallow and extensive thus making access to deeper waters where fish summer difficult.

CRAG LAKE

This is the next lake up the trail from Genevieve, a total distance of slightly less than 5 miles from Meeks Bay. This lake sees few day hikers, as they all seem to poop out at Genevieve 0.4 miles closer to the trailhead. There is a circuitous inlet stream channel from Hidden Lake that is substantially deeper than its surroundings. This channel goes along for a good 200 yards and is certainly worth careful examination. The outlet end of the Lake is rather shallow and not a good bet. One will see browns cruising on the side of the Lake opposite the main trail. These fish are looking for their primary food source, the red-sided shiners that abound in the Lake.

This is not an easy lake to fish and is a good lake for novices to avoid. The browns have an unending food source and are suspicious of imitations. On the other hand, there are large fish. The brown photograph in the Introduction is from Crag and is similar to the one in this Chapter. They spawn in the inlet.

HIDDEN LAKE

This is the next lake up the trail from Crag, about 5.4 miles from Meeks Bay. There is a spur trail from the main trail that leads down to it. One barely catches a glimpse of the lake from the main trail. This appears to be a pure brookie fishery. The outlet area is rather shallow and unappetizing. There are, however, several rocky points and ledges in the lake that attract its residents.

SHADOW LAKE

Just beyond the turn off to Hidden Lake is Shadow Lake. In early morning this lake is in the shadow of Rubicon Peak, hence the name. At this point one is about 6 miles in from the trailhead and really at the limit of feasible (gung-ho) day hiking. Those addicted to reading topo maps will notice that it is only about 2 miles in a straight line to this point from the end of the

First fish Dieter caught in his life....

highest road at the development on Rubicon Bay just south of "Lonely Gulch." This area, however, does not afford access to Shadow Lake, as one cannot reach Forest Service land with trespassing on private property. In any case, this approach would be very difficult at best.

Shadow Lake itself is a reasonable brookie fishery with a few browns thrown in. It is shallow but has good size fish. There is a convenient sand spit next to the inlet stream (in low water) which affords foot access to casting to the inlet stream as well as the lily pads at the entrance side of the lake.

STONY RIDGE LAKE

This large lake is sometimes called "Upper Tallent Lake" but its current name is clearly derived from the 9000' ridge that includes Rubicon Peak and separates it from the Tahoe basin. Stony Ridge Lake has received all types of trout including the first trout plant in the Desolation, mackinaws, in the late 19th century. The largest recorded caught here weighed 28 lbs., but there is little news of any recent catches of this species. The current species likely to be found are rainbows, brookies and browns. There is natural reproduction in the inlet stream.

The center of this lake is over 120' deep, beyond the range of my fish finder. In these deep areas there are few fish to be seen. For those who would like to try to get mackinaw, probably the best advice is to go out with a charter on Lake Tahoe. The definitive reference on mackinaw strategy is by Roush. He has never fished this lake but feels it still contains fish and states he would like to try jigging for them. I have seen large quantities of fish on my fish finder at depths consistent with mackinaw (50-60') but had no success jigging.

The more likely successes in this lake are along the shore at the drop-offs. There are large numbers of fish in this lake but they are difficult to reach without a float tube. A reasonable strategy from the western shore is to try to fish the drop-offs easily visible where the sandy beaches suddenly fall-off to the depths. More rocky drop offs are found on the eastern shore, and these can be reached with relatively short casts from that shore. There are red-sided shiners in the lake and fish move into the shallows for the shiners from the security of these drop offs. One should also note that even when the inlet stream is dry there are springs in the inlet area that attract fish. Fish can also be found up this stream in early summer while there is still flow.

The tactics for fishing this lake are the usual except for those involving mackinaw. The necessities for the Macs are: an inflatable boat or float tube; an early start since they appear to like to feed at daybreak; a fish finder to identify their depth; and large flashy lures, flies or jigs.

Windy day for my wife Danielle at Stony Ridge Lake.

CLIFF LAKE

This small lake is reached from Stony Ridge Lake by a moderate death march up the cross-country track that follows its brushy outlet stream. The lake has extensive cliffs to the southwest. Cliff Lake has innumerable small brookies. Prior attempts to plant goldens failed due to this population of cannibals. Access points are limited due to the terrain, but this does not matter, as there are many (too many) small fish. At least all the rises in the evening are indeed trout and not shiners, as is the case on many other lakes. This is a pleasant camping area a bit off the beaten track. Fish here do not get as large as those of Phipps Lake.

RUBICON LAKE

This is a modest brookies fishery on the trail to Phipps Pass. It is hit rather hard by the passing masses and is a less sure bet than the Grouse or Phipps Lakes.

GROUSE LAKES

These two small lakes are a short distance from Rubicon Lake, but this is a long distance from the Meeks Bay trailhead (8+ miles). Those who spend their winter hours looking at topos will probably have noticed that a gully leads directly up 1.5 miles from Eagle Lake (1 mile from the Eagle Lakes trailhead). This distance is extremely deceptive as the gully is full of large boulders that require climbing skills and alternatives outside the gully require manzanita mountaineering skills of the highest degree. This gully is particularly dangerous to descend (a general rule in technical climbing is that it is easier to go up rocks than down) and one may be forced into some very unpleasant bushes. All in all this "short" approach is a route to avoid.

The Grouse Lakes are brookie lakes. The upper lake was full of up to 12" fish the last time I was there, but fish appeared on the verge of stunting and a bit eel-like. The small lower lake had fewer fish, but the ones I could catch were well-fed and larger than those of the bigger upper lake.

The upper lake has seen beaver activity and their home provides a tenuous casting point for fly and spin anglers. If the lodge disappears, some large boulders behind it allows casting access to a deeper area of the pond that appears to be the lair of its larger residents. The lower lake has some granitic shelves perfect for flyfishing backcasts. The lower lake fish appear to be eating a variety of nymphs in some weed beds but on my last trip they seemed to want to fight over a streamer.

PHIPPS LAKES

General Phipps, a veteran of the Indian wars, settled at the mouth of General Creek near Sugar Pine Campground in Tahoma. His Lakes with its Peak above are well worth a visit. The upper lake is about nine miles from either the Eagle Lakes or Meeks Bay entrance. Again, do not be fooled by the short map distance up the gully from Eagle Lake (see notes on Grouse Lakes). With two cars, one may make a pleasant loop hike up the Eagle Falls Trail past the Velmas and then down the Meeks Bay trail. On such a trip one can (or used to be able to) see some of the most varied fishing in the Wilderness: rainbows in Middle Velma, brookies in Phipps and Grouse Lakes and browns in the Crag Lake area. Because this lake is off the trail- even though only a few hundred yards- it gets less use. The little camp at the outlet has particularly nice views.

Lower Phipps Lake may be reached by a major bushwhacking adventure but has nothing to offer. Over the years I have two reliable reports that Lower Phipps Lake is fishless because it is too shallow. Two parties have suffered the bushwhack in there and cannot confirm earlier stories of lunker brookies- maybe winter-kill got them. Fish still may occasionally descend from the upper lake and stream, but apparently they do not survive long.

This has always been an excellent brookie fishery and the fish have not appeared stunted. If one cannot catch them here, it is hopeless. The lake has also received stocking of goldens, perhaps without the golden supplements they will start looking stunted. Fishing is quite the same all around the lake although there is one excellent granitic shelf that affords casting room for fly fishing. I hope one day to try a bushwhack between Cliff Lake and this Lake. I will make sure that I have an extra battery for my GPS.

The well-rounded female side of the brookie family common in Phipps Lake.

SECTION 6: EAGLE CREEK

The prime access to this area is via the Eagle Lake Trail, but some will use the Bayview trail, which is dusty and steep, but has great views of Emerald Bay. Access to the Snow Lake area on Cascade Creek is via Bayview Campground and the trail leading south from the parking lot. This trail becomes very much cross-country at times and probably receives 5% of the use of the Eagle Lake Trail. You can visit several of these lakes in the same day with an early start and a lot of energy. It is better to descend the Bayview Trail than to climb up it.

EAGLE LAKE

It may be hard to believe that the most heavily used trail and lake in the Wilderness indeed was once surrounded by wild eagle nests. In the distant past both Golden and Bald eagles nested in the high peaks surrounding this picturesque lake. There has been an attempt to reintroduce falcons along the north canyon wall. The lake itself has received rainbows but also has browns and brookies descended via the inlet stream. They must know how to sky-dive to come down this stream.

This view of Lake Tahoe's Emerald Bay is the namesake of the Bayview Trail.

The inlet stream area is the place to fish, along with the area just to the north of the inlet. This clearly can only be done well with a float tube. Surprisingly there are many fish in these areas directly across from where the hordes visit the lake at the point where the trail arrives. One can fish with grasshopper imitations along the bush line and drop-off north of the inlet stream. Nymphs are also effective in the weedy areas bordering the inlet stream. Another interesting place is where the scree slope enters the lake on the north side. The center of the lake is over 80' deep and fishless. There is a little island that is a great place for a float tube picnic. Reports from this lake in 2008 have been enthusiastic about the brown population.

LOWER VELMA LAKE

The Velma Lakes are named after the youngest daughter of Harry Oswald Constock, the manager of the Tallac House resort in the early 1900s. The approved way to reach these lakes is via the excellent trail. Following the stream up from Eagle Lake may look shorter but soon one begins to boulder hop on rocks the size of Volkswagens and this route loses its appeal. The following is the creek that links the Upper and Lower Lakes.

Lower Velma Lake is less visited than the others and has large specimens of the three main trout of the area. The inlet provides for natural reproduction. Several rock shelves provide good flyfishing points. Recent reports have been very positive about this lake throughout the 2000s. I have had particularly good luck floating grasshopper imitations around the lake with a dropper of a small nymph.

MIDDLE VELMA LAKE

This lake is a pure rainbow fishery and the fish achieve some size. There is no natural reproduction due to the lack of suitable spawning areas. One can walk the shoreline and find good sized fish feeding in the shallows and off rocky points. Flyfishing is feasible from many points. There is a, however, lot of area to cover in this lake and a float tube or inflatable boat is extremely useful. Small coves may have large cruising fish. This is another useful lake to have damselfly nymphs and adults available; they may be combined on a dropper with excellent effects. There are large fish here despite the pressure of humanity and this is one lake where ethics suggests catch and release of its larger specimens simply so that more anglers can enjoy them.

In mid-September 1997 I took an overnight to the Velmas. I tested the theory of Heather Lake, i.e. that the wind blows the terrestrials over to the downwind side of the lake. To make a long story short, there are a number of outcroppings of large rocks on the northeast side Middle Velma. There were several rainbows cruising and I landed some 14"-16" on hoppers. I'll not be too specific on the spot, but theory is more important than location -- remember the wind can shift.

If there is one lake that could really benefit from put and grow planting in the Desolation, this is it. It finally received a dose of rainbows in 2007 and there are no frogs here. One can only hope that it does not get an illegal dose of brookies. Reports on the growth of these RT are welcomed. One rise was reported in 2008, so there is hope.

UPPER VELMA AND FONTANILLIS LAKES

Upper Velma, the smallest of the Velmas, is located on the trail up to Fontanillis Lake. There are plenty of brookies in the area and along its outlet and the lakelets downstream. One can get away from the crowds again by following this stream and stalking the wily brookie (You can always pretend it's New Zealand).

Fontanillis is primarily a brook trout fishery and it receives considerable pressure, although recent reports from this lake have been very positive and a 2003 survey found a few large wild rainbows. Upper Velma is off trail and gets less pressure.

The incredible stream connecting Lower and Upper Velma Lakes, a few feet off the trail.

DICKS LAKE

This lake and the associated Peak and Pass are named for the "Hermit of Emerald Bay" Captain Richard Barter. This wild Englishman was a sailor by training and spent much of his time sailing on Tahoe. He unfortunately had a tendency to partake of strong spirits while sailing and one stormy day in 1875 went down with his ship. The Lake which is his legacy was planted with both brookies and rainbows. It receives many visitors due to its proximity to the Pass. The fate of the rainbows planted here is unknown.

GRANITE LAKE

This small Lake (see right) is the one good reason to climb the Bayview Trail. The only other potential reason to climb this dusty trail is the view of Emerald Bay and Eagle Lake from several vantage points. The lake nonetheless has plenty of brookies, but a float tube is almost a necessity due to the overgrown nature of the shore. The biggest fish are found in the spots where it is hardest to cast, at the far side of the lake. There are also a lot of snags and sunken trees at that end.

One may combine a visit to this lake with a visit to Azure Lake as a strenuous but feasible day trip. You can go up the Eagle Lake Trail and then down the Bayview Trail. One can have lunch at Azure and descend to Granite for the evening rise. It is a short jaunt back to the trailhead, but one should bring headlamps or flashlights for this adventure in case one gets carried away with the fishing and becomes "benighted". Unfortunately, there are also

Granite Lake: A quick stumble down the trail at dusk.

many mosquitoes in early season and they are also hungry in the early evening. Recent reports of DFG have shown a drop in the BK population but anglers report tons of fish.

AZURE LAKE

This gorgeous lake (lower right hand corner of the following photo) has gone through a number of name changes. Originally named "Gladys" after the daughter of Harry Oswald Constock, the name appears as "Kalmeia Lake" on the 1945 Forest Service map and the current Kalmia Lake was unnamed. Following the instruction in Wood's guide it can be reached with difficulty from the Cascade Creek area or somewhat more easily from the Eagle Lake or Bayview Trail. Wood's route up Cascade Creek is often wet, requires climbing on steep and slippery rocks and is only for the very sure-footed. Though the trip up the Eagle Lake Trail is a longer distance, the high quality of the trail makes it relatively quick. I would only go up the dusty and steep Bayview Trail to Azure if I intended to stop at Granite Lake on the way back to fish the evening rise. It is also very easy to miss the trail to Azure, which although marked on the topo, lacks a sign on the trail.

This is the way to find it from the Bayview Trail: after passing the saddle between Maggie's Peaks one descends along a ridge. Soon one descends rapidly to the left (south) towards a gully but the trail turns right around a corner. That gully was the trail. Close inspection will reveal that the gully sees considerable human use. A Casio watch altimeter makes it easy to find the trail at the 8240' level. (The Casio used to be a serious backcountry tool until the handheld GPS came along.) If one misses this trail one soon sees the lake and is tempted to go cross-country- better to go back and find the trail rather than fight the bushes.

Though Azure Lake has received some rainbows, the lake itself is a solid brookie fishery with some large fish. The inlet stream provides some aerated water during the summer and is a good spot in hot weather.

SNOW LAKE

This Lake (in the lower left hand corner of the photo) is reached by the cross-country route up Cascade Creek. It's is not hard to get lost in this area though the trail is well-ducked. The lake itself has brookies and there are many points that give access to flyfishing. The fish in this lake appear somewhat stunted and small compared to those in Azure.

For those of you interested in topo maps, take a close look at the inlet area of Cascade Lake, which is private, but is the inlet on private land?

Snow and Azure Lakes are easy to see, but where are Tallac and Kalmia?

TALLAC LAKE

Tallac is from this local Indian dialect "tahlac" for great mountain, and this lake does live in the shadow of Mount Tallac. It had in the 1990s some small surviving golden plants but is very difficult to fish due to a brushy shoreline. Access from Snow Lake should probably best be attempted with a helicopter (To the USFS: I am kidding). It is very tricky to get to Tallac from Snow Lake and the attempt should be avoided due to the steepness of the terrain (see up and left of Snow Lake in the photo). If one gets off the route the consequences could be a serious fall. I can almost guarantee the lake is fishless without the golden plants it used to get. In any case it was very difficult to fish because the banks were covered with willows thereby making casting, retrieval and playing a fish nearly impossible.

KALMIA LAKE

The same access problems exist for Kalmia (does not seem to be visible in the photo). The route mentioned by Wood up its outlet stream is very dangerous due to its steepness and wetness. I found it easier to go these from Snow Lake, but either way is not to be recommended, as this is definitely off trail. Please remember, I used to rock-climb in Yosemite, and do not go up these routes unless you are looking for trouble.

This lake was last stocked in 2004 with goldens and this is planned to continue. Note that DFG netted a 1.5lb specimen out of this lake in 2003 along with 5 other nicely fattened medium-sized fish. I have to say that the setting of this lake is one of the most isolated in the Wilderness.

Middle Velma Lake in the days when it received 10,000 fingerlings a year.

SECTION 7: FALLEN LEAF LAKE

CATHEDRAL LAKE

When one arrives at this small tarn one asks where the cathedral is. The cathedral is represented by the nose of Mount Tallac's southeast ridge which appears to be a formidable mountain from the Fallen Leaf Lake region. The photo is of the Lake during "ice out".

This lakelet did contain goldens in the 1990s who fell for small nymph patterns. As opposed to Cup, there appear to be no scuds. They will take the blown in terrestrial and one often sees rises. The fish are usually small and numbers vary with the success of the DFG bombing run. They do not do well if DFG hits the trees instead of the lake; this is a very small target! The lake probably used to represent the easiest-to-get-to lake with goldens in the Wilderness, but the fish were not big and were quick to scatter. One is rarely alone at this lake due to the traffic up Mt. Tallac and visitors spook the fish. You can flyfish the lake from the far side, as there is casting room. Alternatively, if you have waders, you can fish from the near to the trail side from a shallow area. Wading, however, is a good way to spook these fish. Spin anglers are often frustrated by watching the fish follow without taking the lure. Here the smaller (and perhaps darker) the lure the better. This lake is not easy to fish, but the fish in the lake are a worthy target.

In fall, 1996, the goldens in Cathedral were taking terrestrials on the surface and scuds on a sink-tip. Fish were up to 10". These fish were very hard to catch except in the fall. It seems they become easier to catch just as the lakes start to ice-up and this, of course, is right when we get our first snow and the trails become impassable. It is not clear any fish could have survived without planting and I think this lake is shallow enough to be subject to winter-kill.

FLOATING ISLAND LAKE

To this day matted turf does break off and float about the lake. Unfortunately the huge cutthroat trout that once called this home are long gone. The Lake is hit very hard due to its position on the main trail up Mount Tallac, but it continues to produce plenty of

Cathedral Lake at Ice-Out.

brookies. There are shiners in the lake and streamer patterns work well. One can flyfish with waders from the shallow shore near the trail or use roll casts in several other areas. This is a lake I would like to see restocked with the Lahontan cutthroat that originally lived here. This would provide the passerby with a little bit of the history of the area.

I have fished this lake continuously over the years as it is so close to the road. Many fish are found near

Floating Island Lake, a short hike up the Mt. Tallac Trail. No guarantees that the island is still there.....

the inlet area- my largest over the years has been 13". The fish also cruise the shore across from where the trail comes next to the lake. There is usually a ton of small fish in the center of the lake. This lake is only awkwardly fishable with a flyrod without a tube. Since many fish are near the edge it's better to be in the middle and cast towards the edge. Nonetheless, you can do well roll-casting off the shore. If you do not take a tube, watch-out for the marshy edges near the inlet, as you'll get your feet wet.

GRASS LAKE

Grass Lake is located a couple miles up the Glen Alpine Trail. In past, I reported that it is "overfished and one will have little luck with the few brookies and browns that remain hidden here." How quickly things can change. Another angler visited Grass and Susie in 2003 and reported catching many brookies running 8 to 12 inches, with the larger ones coming from Grass. I spotted even larger ones in the inlet to Grass around 2004. Look for undercuts.

SUSIE LAKE

This lake is either named for one of Nathan Gilmore's daughters or the matriarch of the Washoe Indians. It has a large brookie population with some fish of size. These fish will also take a fly on the surface at dawn and dusk. They are found throughout the lake, but there are good flyfishing areas on rocky points jutting into the lake at several spots. A particularly educational experience in this lake is to examine the inlet stream. It may run underground in

dry years. This "spring" then becomes a major attractor for the population of brookies that are found in this lake. Other lakes have similar "springs" and they are very much worth looking for.

Some additional information is from the 1996 DFG/USFS trip into the Desolation. They camped at Susie Lake to examine a region on the eastern side of the Wilderness for the first time. As I had the feeling from my trip to the area in 1995, probably due to the book, Susie Lake has had its big brookie population decimated. DFG found no fish over 12". This is down substantially from past findings of fish above 16". Nonetheless, Stafford Lehr, DFG biologist, recommends fishing Susie heavily. "... the more fish taken the better, especially those in the range from 8 to 10 inches. We have found that by cropping the population of medium sized fish the larger ones will do better on the numerous forage fish (Lahontan redsides)." More recent reports show a healthy population of BK. Catch and fillet here!

ALTA MORRIS LAKE

In 1993 I wrote that diversity (and frustration) can be obtained at Alta Morris Lake, which allegedly is stocked with goldens. I had yet to see a fish in this lakelet and it is small and clear enough that one can scan virtually every inch. I said that I have had better luck finding scenery than fish at this lake. In 2003 I had a report that found Alta Morris "loaded" with "feisty" brookies that ran to 13 inches. It is not clear to me what they eat in this lake, but perhaps it is the damsels that are so common in Half Moon Lake.

42

HEATHER LAKE

This deep wild Lake is named for the low white and purple heather which border its south end. The Lake is notorious for large trout. These are easier to discuss than land. The brookie population is large and the fish are respectable with many above 12" but it is the browns that are what one would like to catch here. These one may find (Note: find and catch mean different things) in the boulder fields that slide into the lake from the west. Large fish also often lurk along the steep drop-offs right along the trail providing the angler with some spectacular sightseeing. Another interesting area is the inlet area which is best reached by crossing the outlet stream (on some rotten logs) and moving along the shore towards the southwest. As one moves along this shoreline do not neglect the bays and rocky points which are much less often fished than the side of the lake on which the trail is found. There are also some rainbows in here that may use the inlet for spawning. The main reason why these fish are so large is the population of red-side shiners and shiner imitations are clearly the attractor of choice. This lake can be particularly windy and is one of the few lakes where one will be thankful for having a bit heavier equipment. Please note the reference in Woods guide to cross country routes in this area and some of my comments in reference to Triangle Lake.

The problem with Heather is finding the large Browns that are known to live there. The thing is that, every afternoon, there is a good wind from the northwest across the lake. This brings in a lot of insects and terrestrials. The best place to find these insects is on the southeast shore (where they are blown by the wind across the lake). On this particular lake you actually sit at a high point on the southeast shore and watch for fish. Also you can use streamers for the large brookies that are also found in this area. One last thing is that there is a channel right at the outlet with another observation point on the opposite side from the trail (as well as from the trail). Large fish move up and down this channel looking for the red-side minnows on which they feed. I have yet to fully explore the inlet area of the water that comes in from Jack's Peak. It is rather swampy there but I landed a nice fish from the boulder field on the other side of the swamp.

In 1995 Heather was still packed with large fish up to 3 lbs. These fish are tougher to get, as I have said in the past, but there are large brookies and browns to be had. One of the biggest problems for flyfishers remains the difficulty of access with a float tube, so I think these fish will probably be safe. Repeated reports during the 2000s continue to document the existence of big fish with one supposedly to 24" lost at the shore.

The notorious outlet area of Heather Lake where the big browns cruise (one hopes) for minnows.

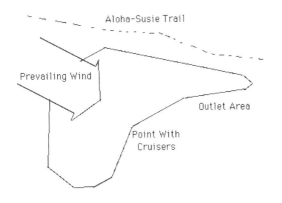

Aloha-Susie Trail

Prevailing Wind

Outlet Area

Point With
Cruisers

Effects of the wind on Heather Lake insect "blow in".

Finally, here's a paraphrase a report from one of our "streamkeepers" who spin fishes and whose e-mail has changed. This angler fished Heather Lake where the Le Conte drains into it, basically at the bottom of the diagram at the left. He had a number of follows on a Kastmaster and landed a "beautiful 14" + brown" which he released. He reported he had a number of lunkers follow his lure without a take. He was "amazed" to see around half a dozen browns just swimming about 5-10 feet from shore. He said that he thought that if he were a flyfisher he would have caught more. As the diagram indicates, this is the point with the cruisers and they are looking up for dry flies (terrestrials). He is absolutely right that they will take the dry cast out into their cruising pattern (when they are not looking at you....).

Cirque or circle of mountains surround Half Moon Lake. Photo by Brianne O'Rourke.

HALF MOON LAKE

This lake is in a wonderful cirque with impressive views. The best campsites are along its south shore. This lake has brookies and rainbows and I believe the rainbows spawn in the inlet stream from Alta Morris Lake. The 1996 DFG survey found that Half Moon Lake had a population of large brookies.

These fish, however, are hard to catch from shore due to the shallow nature of the lake shoreline with large shallow edges with a deeper center. The fish are not at the very shallow edges but along the drop offs into the deeper water- usually some 100' offshore as I recall. Thus, a tube is useful here to get out from the edge. If one is landlocked, one may try some of the deeper shelves that occasionally reach towards the shore. One of the "streamkeepers" of the area, Brian O'Rourke, has fished the flats with his waders and done very well with terrestrials, especially at the outlet area where you would expect them to be drawn. However the best areas are only going to be accessible by float tube- but I would suspect that these fish would be rather naive. Given the difficulty of reaching them, this resource should be safe.

The same "streamkeeper" gave the following report:

"I eventually ended up fishing the outlet stream and lake below which was loaded with brook trout. In the lower area they had their noses into the bank eating damsel nymphs, and if you waited till the wind put a riffle on the water, you could cast in 6 inches of water and get an immediate hookup. At times even some fish would jump out of the water to knock off the adults off the reeds and eat them. I caught well over 12 fish, till the hatch tapered off around 3 in the afternoon."

GILMORE LAKE

Nathan Gilmore first brought cattle and angora sheep to graze in the area around this lake in 1873. On the trail up from Fallen Leaf Lake one will pass through the one time resort village of Glen Alpine (check out the plunge pools in the Creek for browns, brookies and small rainbows). The central attraction of this resort was its spring, which is well identified and the taste of which no doubt contributed to the resort's downfall. Every year I get reports of fish in the area.

Pyramid Peak, the Crystal Range, spring flowers and Gilmore Lake Basin. Photo by Brianne O'Rourke.

Please respect the privacy of the residents of the "village" who have a little historic monument on their hands, which is no doubt a challenge to manage. The old lodge seems to have been partially rebuilt.

The one claim to fame of this lake which is somewhat amusing is that it sports the only gold mine in the area. Anglers with poor luck with the pole can try the pan at the "prospect" located 0.25-0.50 miles directly (true) south of the south shore of the Lake. There is also a very unusual and direct route leading to the lake and this area from near the end of the Lily Lake parking area. Information on this is in Wood's guide. This route is spectacular but only for the sure-footed and those who do not suffer from acrophobia. I have not been up it for years and not sure of its condition.

Gilmore Lake has seen stockings of virtually every species known to man including bass. To no one's surprise brookies do the best, though recently it has received lake trout and large browns also have been taken. This lake is overinhabited by people and I avoid it in full season. One of the few guides who really knows the area, Randy Johnson of Tahoma, fishes the Lake successfully in early season when there are few people and the larger fish surface. With all the alternatives described above, anglers can find better campsites.

Gilmore was also surveyed by DFG in 1996. According to the reports they found a lot of rather stunted (eel-like) 18" lake trout. There were few of other species. Others have reported large fish out of this lake in the past but the

survey could not verify any bigger ones. Stafford still believes there are large fish here best caught with sink-tip lines and minnow imitations off float tubes. John and Judy Wakabayashi proved Stafford right in 2000 and 2001. As you can see from the photo, the Lake Trout are alive and well. According to DFG, there are lots of these fish in the lake and risk getting stunted, hence does not hurt to take a few out. This one looks anything but stunted and is the largest fish I have heard of coming out of the Desolation in decades. Measured at 32" with an 18" girth, my formula comes out with a 12-13 pound fish. The fish may be as many as 20 years old.

John's 12 pound Lake Trout. Photo Judy Wakabayashi.

Also important news from John is that the shortcut in Wood's guide seems to be operational and with good ducking of the trail after you get to the rim. I went up there with a fish finder around 2002-3 and discovered that the lake is at least 195' deep, but did not have John's success. I think that I need to bring my heavy leaded shooting heads next time. As food for thought, a DFG gillnetting party some years ago also found a 10-pound Brown in the Lake. John has a web site with more information on his adventures.

After this fish the couple started having children and at last check they are not large enough to drag up the trail, but I am sure it will not be long before the whole family is back. I have received intermittent reports from this lake over the past few years but nothing to equal this fish, which I think is the "Record" for the Desolation.

CALIFORNIA TROUT'S AGENDA IN THE TAHOE REGION

When I first started out as a "streamkeeper" for California Trout many years ago there were several issues we addressed in the High Sierra: an equitable arrangement to provide habitat for endangered frog species, reducing grazing in the Golden Trout Wilderness and attempting to maintain good water flow in Mammoth Creek on the East Side of the Sierra. CalTrout has always had a policy of staffing small regions or pockets with professionals to manage major conservation issues closely. After careful polling of our members, the Tahoe area was targeted in 2008 to be the next region to staff professionally.

The agenda for this person will, of course, include the Desolation Wilderness and other Wilderness areas close to Tahoe where the issue of trout management will recur. In addition, the streams of the area require attention. The Truckee and its tributaries have no shortage of threats and needs. The problems of Lake Tahoe itself are substantial and long-term. Finally, there are several streams outside the drainage of the Truckee that need attention, such as Silver Creek, the home of the rare and endangered Paiute Trout. Ultimately when the Tahoe office is fully staffed and integrated with already existing staff in the northeastern part of the state (Fall River) and on the East Side (Mammoth) as well as out Wild Trout staff (Sacramento) substantial close-in coverage can be provided for trout issues over much of the Sierra.

CalTrout exists only with the support of its members. Many support with time and effort. Others provide financial help. It is the author's hope that readers of this work will want to get involved with CalTrout. Its web site is always available: http://www.caltrout.org/.

Lake Tahoe by Peter Spain (http://www.peterspain.com).

FREE CALTROUT MEMBERSHIP

Send your receipt from the purchase of this book to: Tahoe/Desolation Membership, CalTrout, 870 Market St., #528, San Francisco, Ca. 94102 for a one-year membership including four issues of the Streamkeeper's Log.

FURTHER READING

Robert Alley: Advanced Lake Fly Fishing: The Skillful Tuber, Frank Amato Publications, Portland, Oregon, 1991.
David N. Cole: Low-Impact Recreational Practices for Wilderness and Backcountry, USFS, Intermountain Research Station, 324 25th Street, Ogden, Utah 84401, General Technical Report INT-265, 1989.
Ron Cordes and Randall Kaufmann: Lake Fishing with a Fly, Frank Amato Publications, Portland, Oregon, 1984.
Ralph Cutter: Sierra Trout Guide, Frank Amato Publications, Portland, Oregon, 1991.
Forest Service, A Guide to the Desolation Wilderness (Forest Service Map), US Department of Agriculture, 1990.
Les Hill and Graeme Marshall: Stalking Trout, Stonewall Press, Washington, D.C., 1985.
Barbara Lekisch: Tahoe Place Names, Great West Books, Lafayette, California, 1988.
Peter Moyle: Inland Fisheries of California, University of California Press, Berkeley, 2002.
John H. Roush: Enjoying Fishing Lake Tahoe, The Truckee River and Pyramid Lake, Adams Press, Chicago, 1987.
Galen Rowell, Galen Rowell's Vision: The Art of Adventure Photography, Sierra Club Books, San Francisco,1993.
Jeffrey P. Schaffer: Desolation Wilderness and the South Lake Tahoe Basin, Wilderness Press, Berkeley, Ca., 1990.
Bill Willers: Trout Biology, Lyons and Burford, New York, 1991.
Robert S. Wood: Desolation Wilderness, Wilderness Press, Berkeley, California, 1975

.

CPSIA information can be obtained at www.ICGtesting.com
Printed in the USA
BVIW12n0004090516
446718BV00006B/45